Who Care

MW00795507

Hassan Ali Jama

Who Cares About
SOMALIA

Hassan's Ordeal

Reflections on a Nation's Future

Verlag Hans Schiler

Contact to the Author:
Hassan Ali Jama
E-mail: *hajama@juno.com*

Cover-photo: Somali village elder,
all Photos: © Herbert Warnke

Distribution:
Verlag Hans Schiler
Fidicinstraße 29
D-10965 Berlin
Tel. +49-30-322 85 23
Fax. +49-30-322 51 83
E-mail: info@verlag-hans-schiler.de
www.schiler.de

© Verlag Hans Schiler, Berlin
All rights reserved
1. Edition 2005
Edited by Herbert Warnke
Layout: textintegration.de
Cover-design: JPP Berlin
Printed in Mongolia

ISBN 3-89930-075-0

Table of Contents

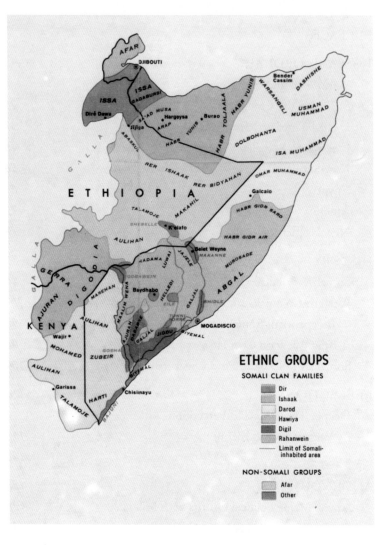

ETHNIC GROUPS

SOMALI CLAN FAMILIES

- Dir
- Ishaak
- Darod
- Hawiya
- Digil
- Rahanwein
- —— Limit of Somali-inhabited area

NON-SOMALI GROUPS

- Afar
- Other

Preface

This book is about the Somali civil war and the fall of the Siad Barre regime. It is about how people living there at the time did really suffer from it as a result.

Although it principally relates to a family that is considered one of the relatively fortunate ones which survived the ordeal of undergoing the civil war in the African Continent at the onset of the 1990's during the twentieth century at the heels of the Rwandan massacre and immediately preceding the ouster of the Ethiopian dictator, Menghistu Haile Mariam of Ethiopia.

It is about the political history of Somalia and about Somali ethnicity in general. The book also discusses the future of the Nation and how international and regional powers are involved in playing their sometimes influential roles in its intricate and complicated political path.

It makes a cautious suggestion that it rests on Somalis themselves to shoulder their own future. It mentions carefully that the present generation, including the author, has failed to provide an amicable solution so far to its seemingly intractable debacle and asks them to find a successful formula even by hindsight out of the mess the country found itself in.

It also asks the new generation to provide forward looking ideas, formulae or solutions to bring back the nation up to its feet and its deserving place in the right course of history.

Now that the reconciliation conference amongst Somali tribes, which was being held in neighboring Kenya for the last two years with both regional and international support, have finally agreed to select an interim Federal National Assembly and a National President, one sincerely hopes that the resulting Somali administration shall eventually succeed to adequately reestablish peace and unity for a nation of which both were dismantled or partially disappeared in the aftermath of the civil war of January 1991.

In a nutshell, this is the basic subject of the book. For Somalis, international observers, historians and scholars alike one hopes these few lines shall offer some ideas to ponder and some more food for thought.

This book also extensively describes the very kind and warm welcome the family received from the good people of Washington State, especially by my true friends David and Karen Axe who tried their best to make my life continue as sustainable and solvent as in the Middle East and who also welcomed us to Seattle, and by Mark and Katie Muhsam who gave me shelter, impeccable hospitality and who also provided my family with the right material and atmosphere to be able to achieve our goal of realizing a respectable living in this State.

It also sufficiently mentions several aspects of life in the North West and the beautiful scenery enjoyed by the population of King and Snohomish counties of Western Washington.

My special thanks must be pointed out for Dave Axe, Herbert Warnke and Prof. Dr. Jörg Janzen who assisted me in releasing this work to the reader. They also go to whoever assisted me knowingly or unknowingly to research and choose the correct material for this book

Naturally my special thanks also go to my wife Khadija and to my son Ahmed who spent a sizeable amount of their time assisting me throughout in realizing my aim and without whose contribution this work could not have been carried out to the satisfaction of the undersigned and hopefully of the reader.

Hassan Ali Jama

Hassan's Ordeal

War, Flight and Friends

It was one wintry morning on New Year's Day 1991, when residents of Mogadishu were awakened by the rocking sounds of cannon fire, deafening grenade explosions and whizzing screeches of bullets, hitting and exploding everywhere, sparing no living soul and no object from people to buildings. No one was safe. Nothing was immune.

Winter in Mogadishu, contrary to what might one expect, is not the cool, tropical breeze, nature bestows on the Indian Ocean's African coast this time of the year, or which engulfs the atmosphere after the torrid, humidity laden rains of autumn, as is the norm in most sub-Saharan climates.

Instead, the weather delivers a mixture of sandy north-easterly trade winds and sticky humid heat waves, which blow cold spells of, out of the blue, sandy winds late at night to early dawn, then turn into hot, searing gusts during daylight hours, punishing pedestrians and anyone who ventures outdoors.

It is also the time of the year during which the onslaught of respiratory infections invade Mogadishu and its surrounding region lavishly infesting the environment, causing tremendous health hazards to the feeble, infants and elderly alike as well as to the able bodied.

Hell broke loose all of a sudden, but for most Mogadishu residents it was more of an escalation of the intermittently violent militant insurgency by tribal militias against an oppressive Military autocratic regime that had fallen out of favor. The population had become accustomed to scattered battles for the last two years, but it was now full scale rebellion with a final outcome no one could predict.

For Hassan, like many other Somali citizens residing in the Capital, this will turn out to be the most shocking experience of his life. When he opened his eyes to the shattering noise of cannon fire, he immediately sensed disaster has finally struck home.

He was also aware this civil war will leave no one unscathed. So complex and diverse, it may drag on for decades due to the ignorance of even its own perpetrators of its consequences and worse even due to the ignorance of neutral foreign, if there exist any, mediators or arbiters of its real causes and of its sensible solution.

A multitude of conflicting ideas and thoughts raced through his troubled mind. The most urgent and realistic idea was to keep his mind focused on facts on the ground. As horrible as those facts were, he decided to immediately consult his wife and confer with the rest of his immediate kin as a first step and then act on whatever decision the whole family may decide.

Residential estates in Mogadishu

Things were not going the way they should, however. Dodging all sorts of crisscrossing fire-power kept interrupting normal human activity. The whole day was spent mostly, in either continuous flurry of keeping children indoors, making or answering urgent phone contacts and consulting through which, more friends and kinsfolk, often ducking to the ground whenever a mortar launched missile was sighted heading toward the Towfiq neighborhood.

These mortar rounds came from the Presidential Palace or "Villa Somalia" where the presidential elite security forces, otherwise known as the notorious "Red Berets", were dug in, in a final desperate effort to defend their besieged stronghold, soon to be overwhelmed and overrun by insurgent tribal militias and rebellious masses.

What made our neighborhood a prime target for the Red Berets' guns was the unfortunate choice of nearby Hotel Towfiq, one of the newly built modern hotels in the capital, as one of the strategic command posts by the insurgent militia leadership.

At least twelve mortar missiles flew over Hassan's stone-built, concrete roofed, one storied house, hitting and demolishing nearby, mostly corrugated roofed abodes, annihilating innocent citizens, including women, children often hitting at innocent pedestrians treading the dirt alleys and snake trails in the back streets of the neighborhood only one or two blocks away from Hassan's residence.

More than twenty-five mortar shells also hit the nearby asphalt main "Nr. 30" street, only one block to the south from where Hassan's house stood.

Just over twenty persons who gathered hurriedly to exchange news of the latest development at the junction on the eastern corner of the Towfiq hotel were struck and instantly wiped out by a volley of early morning mortar missiles specifically aimed at the hotel. The hotel itself miraculously escaped damage.

Concurrent to the mortar shelling from the Presidential Palace another battle was raging on between an army contingent, holed in Mogadishu's Chinese built new Central Stadium, across the street just beyond two blocks to the west from Hassan's abode, and bands of militia insurgents who penetrated the north-western part of the Capital after outflanking and overrunning Military strategic posts and were further inflated by massive crowds of frustrated anti-regime mostly tribal oriented youth, who were already equipped with their own rifles and were battle ready.

This battle made any movement, outside homes in all the Towfiq area adjacent to the stadium, impossible. Crisscrossing gunfire from all sides and from all sorts of automatic weapons were occupying whatever airspace left by the endless volleys of rocket missiles flying willy-nilly from all directions, signaling certain death or serious injury for anyone who ventures outside his or her doorstep.

Fierce gun duels subsided after sunset, however. Total darkness fell on the moonlit city, like a dark curtain folding on the first episode of a tragic saga, befitting the gloomy day's diabolic events. Citizens were, nevertheless, accustomed to darkness having experienced years of energy blackouts as a trade mark of declining government efficiency and despicable economic blunders. Yet it was a respite of sorts. People will, at least, be able to focus on planning how to get themselves and/or their loved ones out of this deadly trap.

It was during these precious dark but relatively quiet (except for the distant gunfire sounds) hours, that Hassan and his family decided to move out of their home and temporarily stay in his close friend Dr. Abdi's house near the "Km 4" area where the security situation was relatively less threatening for the initial period.

The plan was to pack everything needed for the trip overnight and depart on foot early at dawn the next day before missiles start to fly again. Once there, Hassan was to immediately look for transport to move a group of 18 persons, including some neighbors. Although to find a vehicle and a driver in these circumstances was next to impossible.

It was not enough. One had to find a trustworthy armed escort or buy an automatic or semiautomatic rifle or preferably a machine gun without which the vehicle shall be confiscated and its occupants simply eliminated.

The rule of the gun was already in force. That same evening the neighbors across the street, a recently married couple came over to spend the night at Hassan's. They could not trust their corrugated roofed house lest an erratic missile hit them in the dark. Both families shared their woes and anxieties. The catastrophic events did plant a pessimistic feeling in everybody's mind. The future of the nation as a whole was in jeopardy.

Hassan's family adult members and their guests almost stayed awake the whole night. The anxieties, it seems, were stronger than the need to rest after a really tiresome day.

No sooner than dawn light presented itself, everybody in the household sprang up ready for the march. One of the children peaked at the road in front of the house and was amazed at the spectacle of the enormous masses of people leaving their houses and crossing the streets carrying a paraphernalia of household items heading to supposedly safer havens.

She could not contain her amazement and yelled at the top of her voice "Mom, come and have a look. Everybody is running away. Neighbors are leaving. Here is aunt Ibaado, there is uncle Geelle".

At this point her mother shot back. "Shut up, lest the people hear you" and she approached the same peaking hole, from the front living room window, facing the street to satisfy her own curiosity.

Hassan was thinking of the safest route to take on the way to Km 4. There were several areas to cross that were all fraught with peril.

The most dangerous were the crossing from the Sinai market to the Hararyaale flea market which is directly to the north of the Presidential Palace and part of the extended Wardhiigley quarter. On the first day this crossing and its surroundings the area received the largest share of canon missiles in a futile attempt by the "Red Berets" to prevent insurgents from taking this direct and easy asphalt road in their final assault at the Palace.

Mogadishu theatre and library

The second perilous point was only half a mile to the west. Unofficially dubbed "Tokyo" by the populace, it was heavily infested with militias from the Central Region loyal to General Aideed who have been locked in a war of attrition with the regime's armed forces for the past two years.

Tokyo was a thorn in the flesh of the local Police for the last few months. Some of the Police senior officers in Mogadishu, faced with the unwillingness of junior officers and the rank and file to carryout foot patrols in the narrow alleys of that specific area where they were turned into easy targets for shadowy militia snipers after sunset, have limited their security details to daylight assignments, continuing harassment of the households who were under constant suspicion of providing shelter to the elusive militia operatives because of their shared tribal affiliations.

Now that hostilities have openly flared up in the Capital, mortar bases and mounted anti-aircraft placements and other defensive entrenchments and barriers suddenly mushroomed turning the area into a battlefield.

The idea of crossing these danger fields prior to sunrise seemed to be the best option in the circumstances, however. Hassan and the family with several escorts from the neighborhood began their march as planned.

The fact that almost everybody in the north eastern part of the Capital was moving out of the area did make the march similar to an exodus. The streets were crowded but not yet overcrowded. Hassan had mixed feelings about the crowded streets and mass departure from the town by the civilian residents. In a way it inspired apprehension that a kind of an Armageddon is taking place. On the other hand, he tacitly enjoyed the company of so many fellow humans in the flight of danger.

As Hassan's entourage headed toward Km 4, he noted the total absence of uniformed Police and Military from the streets. Instead an assortment of town youth volunteers, later dubbed "Mooryaan", each armed with a rifle and United Somali Congress (USC) militia insurgents armed with automatic Kalashnikovs and some loaded with mobile rocket launchers "Bazookas" squatted on pavements and on thresholds of private homes cheerfully smiling to the departing residents, and were showing up V signs.

Apparently pleased at the fact the militia insurgency finally reached the Capital, breaking through the Military strategic check-points the regime had established at the northwestern edges of the city. Neither the squatting militant youth nor their USC leadership knew what was in store for them and for the nation they claimed to rescue.

Two minutes after Hassan and family along with the other crowds went past the Sinai-Hararyaale crossing a volley of missiles was delivered by the Red Berets. The Tokyo area they were approaching was suddenly abuzz with militant operatives' activity who started preparing themselves for a long day. They began eying passing crowds with suspicion. But the clan based singling out of individuals and the ethnic cleansing which became common later on was not in force as yet. Hassan and company continued their march through Tokyo unhindered.

Mogadishu gold-market

As they reached the temporary battlefront dividing line between the opposing sides at the Hawl Wadaag crossing, they met with the first real shock. A burnt out armored car with half a dozen corpses of Military officers lay about at the narrow crossing point. A clear evidence of a successful ambush by the insurgents who put their shoulder held Bazookas to effective use on yesterday's confrontation with the armed forces.

Hassan momentarily surveyed the awe stricken faces of his five children especially that of his five year old daughter who clutched his wrist in horror, and wondered what impact the traumatic effect of this horrible scene may have on the poor child.

A recurrence of similar scenes was encountered by the family before finally arriving at their temporary address near Km 4.

Dr. Abdi's house was only two blocks away from Banadir High School and directly facing Sheikh Ali Suufi Middle School. This area was relatively quiet during the first month of the civil war whilst the regime's armed forces were still desperately trying to defend Siad

Barre who was inexplicably reluctant to leave Villa Somalia and was broadcasting unbelievable reports of the situation in the Capital.

But as Hassan's family barely settled in their new residence, Hassan discovered another ugly face of the war.

The armed forces have apparently been looting all the valuables from residences abandoned by expatriate tenants who mostly inhabited there and of the wealthy and middle class nationals who happened to live in this part of the city.

Shortly after, Hassan joined some friends living in the area as they gathered in a nearby friend's house. A neighboring physician was describing how a soldier whom he had successfully treated in earlier days told him that he was doing him a favor by sparing his life and only carting off a worthless refrigerator. He believed, the doctor commented, sarcastically, he was being magnanimous by looting his property and allowing him to live for another day.

Arabic style house in Shangani

Whilst the friendly ad hoc gathering were engaged in exchanging stories related to the new ominous developments, the neighboring abodes, some of which, already vacated by their inhabitants, were actually being looted by members of the armed forces. Some one in the group noted the worst is yet to come.

The rebel's propaganda machinery was also busy spreading all kinds of stories discrediting the regime to counter the false picture Radio Mogadishu portrayed.

Apart from the false rumors and counter rumors which were rife in the Capital amidst the hostilities, an important incident occurred at the main armory of the highly trained paramilitary Police Force locally called "Daraawish" or the Dervishes after the famous liberation war leader Mullah Mohamed Abdulle Hassan's army at the birth of the 20th century.

A crowd of rebellious town youth broke into the aforementioned armory and took hold of thousands of assorted weapons including rifles, machine guns and rocket launchers, erroneously believed by the populace to have been donated by the Federal Republic of Germany in the past.

The correct version of the matter was that based on an agreement between the German Ministry of Defense and the Somali Police Force, the Federal Republic of Germany have continued to provide the Police Force with multidimensional nonmilitary assistance in the form of means of transportation (trucks, patrol cars and sedans for the top brass) plus communication services, fire fighting and energy generating equipment, it also included construction of Police housing, vocational training in German institutes and educational training in Germany especially in the medical and engineering fields without interruption since 1962. It remains unknown until today how this arsenal ended up in the Daraawish armory.

This incident, however, resulted in availing immense supply of weaponry and munitions to the arms hungry youth supporters of the USC. To its present detriment the Military Regime had been implementing a long term program of training all young Somalis of middle to high school age for country defense purposes since the end of the Somali-Ethiopian war of 1977/78.

Consequently, breaking into the vast and well preserved cache of the Police arsenal may have contributed to tipping the balance in favor of the militias and sympathizers of the USC in the crucial battle for the control of the Capital.

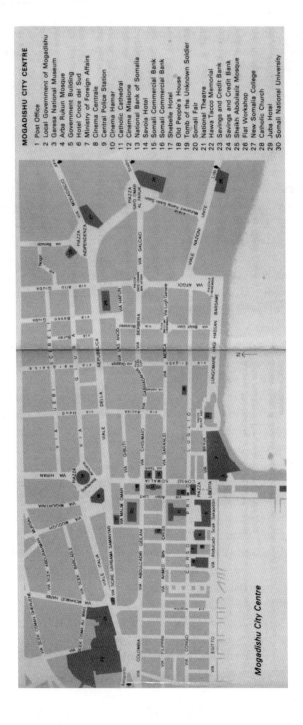

MOGADISHU CITY CENTRE

1 Post Office
2 Local Government of Mogadishu
3 Garesa National Museum
4 Arba Rukun Mosque
5 Government Building
6 Hotel Croce del Sud
7 Ministry of Foreign Affairs
8 Cinema Centrale
9 Central Police Station
10 Cinema Hamar
11 Catholic Cathedral
12 Cinema Missione
13 National Bank of Somalia
14 Savoia Hotel
15 Somali Commercial Bank
16 Somali Commercial Bank
17 Shebelle Hotel
18 Old People's House
19 Tomb of the Unknown Soldier
20 Somali Fair
21 National Theatre
22 Hawa Tacco Memorial
23 Savings and Credit Bank
24 Savings and Credit Bank
25 Sheikh Abdulaziz Mosque
26 Fiat Workshop
27 New Somalia College
28 Catholic Church
29 Juba Hotel
30 Somali National University

Mogadishu City Centre

Hassan's efforts to find safe transport notwithstanding, he began losing hope of either finding his friends in the armed forces who, understandably, could not be located in the circumstances or getting a mini-bus to Afgoi at any fare. He asked his family and company to pack up for a long trek to Afgoi approximately 23 km to the west.

Hard as this decision was, it was the only option open to him. To endure a long trek by foot to the country side was a safer bet than wait for things to deteriorate in Mogadishu.

Whilst briefly staying with his family at his friend's abode near Banadir High School he observed other Mogadishu residents moving en masse toward the country side.

One of the heart rending sights was that of a middle aged man carting his disabled frail mother on a construction cart, the type used to haul stones and dirt on construction sites in the absence of any other affordable means of transport. Hassan offered him and his mother drinking water which he made available to all passers-by who were forced to move by the ongoing hostilities out of their homes.

The man thanked Hassan for the water and told him that whilst his wife accompanied the children to his brother's house in Wadagir district further to the south west of the city also by foot and might have made it there already, it might take him one more hour to arrive at his brother's home because of the difficulty in moving the cart through the mostly dirt streets.

The exodus-like departure from town continued in the first few days without any violent incidents except for few car accidents by scurrying Military personnel moving out of the Capital along the Afgoi highway that links Mogadishu to the western and southern provinces of the country. But other crowd movement related incidents like mothers delivering or undergoing labor pains by the highway side dirt pavement were abound and just normal.

Everybody was on the run it seemed, some planning to return after hostilities did come to an abrupt end. Others called it quits and intended to land where destiny took them.

After Hassan waited with the family at Km 7 in the hope of finding the now turned golden Afgoi - Mogadishu route minibus for about an hour, he agreed with his wife Khadija to dash back home and make sure to deliver the house keys to his friend and continue his search for transport at least for the day.

Hassan walked back home along the dirt pedestrian path passing by the American Embassy compound which later had become the Headquarters for the ill fated UNOSOM intervention force and watched the US Navy choppers shuttling in and out of the compound and moving US and other diplomatic expatriates to the safety of a US aircraft carrier moored in the Indian Ocean waters outside Mogadishu harbor.

At the time, Hassan thought, as he glimpsed some diplomatic personnel from various European Embassies he knew through his travel agency business, entering the compound gate, it was a timely effort to save all foreigners from what is essentially a local political conflict turned into civil war.

Hassan was not aware of how events will eventually unfold to warrant an international intervention and a doomed one at that in the Somali intractable political quagmire.

As he arrived back at the transit home of his benevolent friend and barely waited for one hour, his friend Mahmoud "Salteye", a Mogadishu born ex-colleague from his days at Somali Airlines, came riding his "Piaggio" scooter and gave Hassan a snack breakfast he miraculously grabbed in an obscure restaurant in Ceel Gaab, the popular downtown quarter. Salteye apparently met Hassan's family as they started their trek toward Afgoi.

In a brief conversation with Khadija he invited the whole family to his country cottage near Moallim Noor's public cemetery at Km 14 to which Khadija apologized. She also gave him Hassan's current address.

True to his typically generous character, he decided not to come empty handed to see his friend and to renew his offer to host Hassan's family despite his modest means in these uncertain times. Although Hassan left employment with Somali Airlines nearly a decade ago his friendship with Salteye remained intact.

Salteye trusted his friend and kept his savings from remittances of his own daughters who were striving as domestic workers in Italy with the travel agency under the personal care of his friend.

No one trusted Somali banks during the declining years of the Siad Barre regime. The public became fully aware their deposits were being used to fund endless wars of attrition with tribal militias in various regions of the country and almost boycotted local banks.

In fact Hassan took the extra precaution and kept Salteye's deposits in his own personal safe to be always within easy reach whenever Salteye needed it. Hassan saw Salteye's surprise visit on the scooter as a golden opportunity to deliver him his savings from the agency's office down town.

After ascertaining it was still relatively safe to reach the office Hassan asked his friend to give him a lift to the office to grab some cash. Except for some early morning mortar shelling into the Shangaani and Ceel Gaab areas, no actual combat has occurred as yet in the down town areas.

Looting was gaining momentum however mostly by the crowds. Looters sensing that the Police and armed forces had their hands full in battles with the militias in other parts of the city ventured looting the local branch of the Somali Commercial Bank at Sharif Abbo, various private shops and other properties.

Savoi Center

Hassan and Salteye arrived at Savoy Center where his office was located on the first floor facing the Central Bank. Everything was still in tact, the building, ground floor shops and upper level offices and apartments. Even the armed Police contingent was still guarding the Central Bank. It was too early yet for the militias to overrun Siad Barre's last defenses. It was about noon when Salteye dropped Hassan at his friend's house.

Around 11 a.m. the next morning Dr. Abdi came by accompanied by Dr. Mohamed Ali "Mini-Mini" in a Military truck replete with an armed guard.

Hassan thanked God in silence only his face could not hide his delight at how things are turning to the better after the ominous start the day before, of early morning trekking to Km 7 with family members among the fleeing masses, hoping against heavy odds to find transport, at whatever price drivers demanded, to the temporary safety of Afgoi.

Hassan welcomed his friends, his face beaming with a smile betraying his happiness at their sincere effort to lift their friend out of his helpless situation. They were true guardian angels for Hassan or at least this is how he viewed them at that particular moment.

After Hassan informed them that the family is trekking by foot to Afgoi, Dr. Mini-Mini asked Hassan, with urgency reflecting the tightness of available time, to board the truck and try catch up with Khadija and the children.

Dr. Mini-Mini was promoted to a full Colonel to become the top officer of the Medical Corps of the Somali Army only one year ago, but way before that, Dr. Mini-Mini and Hassan knew each other very well. Both, along with Dr. Abdi and few other physicians including Dr. Abdurahman Onaaye and Dr. Osman Aden, belonged to a larger social group that transcended tribal affiliations and used to meet at a friend's house near Km 4.

Hassan remembered that evening of May 1985 when they visited Banadir Maternity Hospital and arranged along with Dr. Mohamed Jama Baydhabo a special room for Khadija and the infant immediately after his daughter Anisa was born. These guys, he gratefully confirmed to himself, are still carrying-out their role as his rescuers in times of need.

Hassan boarded the truck which hit the Mogadishu-Afgoi highway in no time. After half an hour of high speed driving they spotted Khadija with several other adult members of her companions walking by the roadside dirt pathway about quarter a mile west of Lafoole Teachers Training Institute compound.

After the whole group spent the night as guests with their hosts, Khadija and one of her hosts managed to rent a donkey-cart from a village neighbor at the inflated fare of Somali Shilling (So.Sh.) 50.000. In normal times, the fare would be So.Sh.50 only; but in war time there is no room for bargain. The elderly and the children were bundled onto the cart to the Afgoi address they were heading to.

Khadija and her companions squeezed into the truck and the whole group continued their high speed drive to Haawo Taaco area where the children had already arrived. The speeding truck got to the Afgoi address in a very short time. Hassan, Khadija and their group were dropped. Hassan's friends dashed back to Mogadishu with the truck after completing their mission of moving Hassan and family out of harms way.

But for Hassan only the first part of the ordeal was over. He had to continue trekking toward the village of Adalay, 12 miles north of Afgoi. Afgoi itself was not regarded as a safe place. It has been taken over by Colonel Omar Jess' militia who entered the town from the Bay area after being engaged in skirmishes with government Military contingents there and after overrunning the small unit guarding the Ballidoogleh airbase, whilst the incumbent institutions, although crumbling, belonged to the besieged administration of Siad Barre.

It was also a passageway for armed fleeing government soldiers who were looting everything their hands could grab on the way.

Jess himself was a staunch ally of General Aideed. Moments after he entered the town, he established himself in the Presidential Palace which for many years was reserved for the President of the United Arab Emirates after he paid a state visit to Somalia during the late seventies. The palace was being supervised by an employee of the Ministry of Tourism. Employees were paid by the embassy of the United Arab Emirates.

As Hassan and family were waiting for their host in Adalay to arrive, he ventured to visit the palace where he was told that many of his friends from Mogadishu were already staying as guests prior to the colonel's arrival. All of them fled the war and were heading to safety. During his visit to the palace compound he heard that Colonel Jess just had a meeting with some selected members from various fleeing groups who complained to him of the ethnic cleansing being implemented by the USC and by Aideed's militias. He told them, since they tolerated Siad Barre's torture of the Somali people for two decades, they can withstand the present turmoil for few more days until Siad Barre is ousted. The group left him disappointed and disheartened.

Few days later Aideed's followers drove him and his militia out of Afgoi and chased him until he reached Kismayo where he reigned for a while.

Shelter in the Countryside

Around noon on the third day of their stay in Afgoi, Hassan's host in Adalay Warsama and his son Sheikh Noor arrived to their address in Afgoi, with two donkey carts. The address in Afgoi belonged to Warsama's niece Hawo Moallim, whose husband was actually in Saudi Arabia as one of the Somali laborers who fled the unemployment ridden Somali economy to support their families back home.

Although the four room stone house she owned and lived in with her two children was already packed with guests fleeing the battle raging in nearby Mogadishu, she showed no sign of being inconvenienced and welcomed the additional burden of the new guests with open heart and gregarious spirit.

In her younger days before she got married, she lived with her aunt in Mogadishu for many years. Her aunt was the eldest member of Hassan's group. She regarded the incoming guests as the branch of her extended family, moving out of civil war in the Capital to the temporary safety in Afgoi and other smaller towns and hamlets.

Hawo thought but was not sure, like most others, matters will improve after the battle in Mogadishu comes to its inevitable end.

In the same morning Hassan escorted three ladies who were part of his group from Mogadishu to the bus stop station for Qoryooley, 60 km to the south. Two other ladies of the neighborhood were also escorted to the same bus station heading for Jannaale 40 km to the south, which would be their temporary refuge.

Khadija and the remaining ladies began to pack for the continuation of their trek. That they were leaving at noon under the scorching heat posed no problem for the adults in the family. They were used to this equatorial climate. They were not apprehensive about theft and that of children kidnapping either. The country side path leading to Adalay was deemed to be secure, barring no surprises.

The children, the elderly and the weak climbed on the two carts for the 12 mile ride through thin bush and corn farms. For the children this was a joy ride, compared to the trip between Lafoole and Afgoi three days ago where they all had to precariously squeeze into one cart along with the elderly and hold to each other whenever a speeding truck whizzed by.

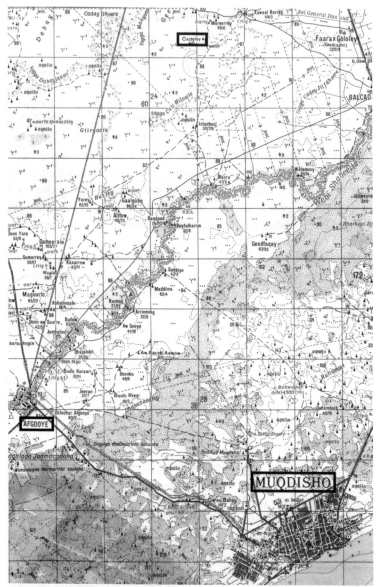

From Mogadishu to Afgoi to Adalay

Mahmoud, 10 years old and the eldest son of the children, decided to walk the whole remaining part of the trek. He was so enthusiastic and energetic; he was always about 100 meters ahead of the donkey cart caravan.

On the way to Adalay the caravan passed by two villages. As they approached the second village there came two men armed with rifles. They gave the usual "nabad miyaa" (is there peace) greeting and moved on.

Warsama told Hassan, the men were from nomadic tribes in the area. At their worst, they sometimes harass young girls returning from Afgoi to their farms at this time of the day for any cash they may carry after selling farm produce including milk in Afgoi. The weapons they carry on their shoulders are necessary for their own safety and for the protection of their camel herds.

Although only forty kilometers from the Capital, life was still peaceful. Hassan wondered silently how long it will take the hostilities taking place there to reach the surrounding country side. The fall out of the Mogadishu city life is already being felt here. His family's flight to Adalay was part of it he knew.

Neither Hassan nor his host Warsama could predict how long the troubles in the Capital will last and whether they will remain confined to Mogadishu or whether they will spread to engulf the whole nation but they both prayed to the almighty for hostilities to come to a quick end.

After the caravan passed by Lafagaalo village, Adalay suddenly appeared in the horizon. It was a quarter a mile away. It took approximately three and half hours for the group to arrive there.

Upon arrival at Warsama's residence in Adalay, Hassan and Khadija observed, adverse prevalent state of affairs notwithstanding, the great effort Warsama and his household made to prepare for receiving the town based relatives arriving in their midst after fleeing the hostilities in the Capital.

Two entire cottages were reserved for the incoming folks. A separate septic rest room had been erected to account for the incoming guests needs. It appeared Warsama took care of all contingencies within his means.

The group disembarked and dispersed into their cottages. Hassan and Khadija read a solemn prayer and thanked God for their safe arrival all in one piece to their temporary refuge and prayed for those still remaining in the Capital to be saved from the senseless violence still raging in Mogadishu.

Khadija was then advised by the lady host Sitey that lukewarm fresh water was ready for each of the arriving group to take bath after a long and tiresome journey. Such was the magnificent generosity of the Somalis in the countryside that it surpassed all cost minded urban dwellers' standards.

Young Somali woman

By sunset Hassan, Warsama and Sheikh Noor went to the village mosque to join other villagers for the usual daily sunset worship. Walking back home about 120 meters they all sat with younger sons of Warsama for a feasty dinner opened with prayers by Warsama, followed by a brief word of appreciation from Hassan for the great effort and sacrifice demonstrated by Warsama and his family.

Conversation and chatter continued for about one hour when time for night worship came up. For this purpose mats were placed underneath a large Mango tree within the perimeter of the residence. A medium sized lantern was also conveniently placed nearby on the ground to provide a modicum of lighting for the worshippers.

After the night worship was completed everybody retired. Farmers have to retire early, since they get up at daybreak and start work immediately after conducting their worship and prayers. They may sip one cup of coffee before setting off to the farm, but they normally plan to take their breakfast during a short break at about ten o'clock in the morning. Citizens of the southern farming belt of Somalia are coffee consumers as opposed to the predominantly tea drinking nomads of the north.

In their first morning at Adalay, Khadija and the elder two of her daughters accompanied the other females in Warsama's household to fetch drinking water from the village reservoir.

Hassan learned there is a Qur'anic school in the village and set out to meet the teacher to apply for enrolling all the kids excluding infants. One of the advantages of living in a small village is the closeness of things to each other and to home.

Since in poor countries many important essential services are available only in towns where both income and size of citizenship can generate enough taxes, only services locally organized by the village or hamlet community, like building a water reservoir or a small mosque, are available in small villages.

Qur'anic school teachers normally conduct their classes in their own huts. After arranging for kids to join the Qur'anic classes, Hassan joined Warsama at his main farm two miles to the north.

One of the realities of village life is the absence of modern methods of transport. On the way to the farm Hassan had to pass by two isolated graves on the right side of the dirt pathway. Out of respect for the dead he read two or three short Suras from the Qur'an. It took him twenty five minutes to reach the farm. It was 10.00 am.

He found Warsama sitting with two middle aged farmers under a large shady tree apparently discussing some private matters. Hassan gave them the necessary customary greeting. Warsama and his guests stood up and courteously invited him to join them. Hassan politely apologized for the moment to allow them continue their private talk and agreed to join them after he had acquainted himself with the farm.

As Adalay was at least 12 miles away from Afgoi it had no share of the irrigation system of canals fed by the Shabelle River to closer villages and hamlets. Farms like Warsama's depended basically on rain water. Even for the farms which are lucky to be part of the irrigation system it was seasonal and could only be relied upon after rain in the Ethiopian highlands flood the Shabelle River until it over-flows. If the rains fail to materialize, it becomes a guessing game.

Water sipping camels

Farming in the village was essentially for subsistence. Corn being the main staple of food in the river area and its neighboring villages of Bay, Banadir plus parts of Hiran, it constituted the bulk of farming work. The excess crops of the seasonal harvest are sold to brokers at the local market in nearby Afgoi for family cash needs.

One could easily note from conversations with village residents the quasi total absence of government support who for many years were engaged in political jugglery and machiavellian tactics with the sole aim to remain in power by whatever means possible, neglecting in the process the basic services required to answer the true needs of the populace.

Warsama had a big family including himself, wife Sitey, six sons and one daughter. The eldest son Sheikh Noor, an austere young man of 21, of pious and religious outlook, hence the title "Sheikh", was assisting his father work the farm and in charge of conducting family finances. He was preparing himself to get married and start his own family soon.

Mohamed, the second eldest son, was in charge of overseeing work at the second family farm, located about three and half miles to the west of the village. Both farms occupied a total of three and a half acres. The smaller farm was partly cultivated with corn and to a smaller degree with vegetables.

Aweis, the third in line of seniority, and Mumin were responsible for herding cattle to pasture in the open country side field and to bring them back by sunset everyday.

Abdi Garas was still in the Qur'anic school. Jibril, barely beyond his toddler age, was wiling his days by building mud castles not far from his mom's sight.

The only daughter, Amina, was a pillar of support for her mother in carrying out the burdensome domestic chores catering for as big a household as Warsama's.

The excess of the vegetable and dairy produce was sold at the Afgoi market for small cash needs. In addition to deftly and dexterously managing his farms and large family in an enviably quiet and efficient manner, Warsama was also the traditional head of the village to whom all elders sought council and sometimes mediation in settlement of disputes. He also carried his responsibilities in this capacity with admirable sense of justice and efficient dispatch.

With all these attributes to his credit, Warsama did not exude an aura of authority, a characteristic generally noticed in Somali elders who hold similar positions and enjoy the same social status, certainly not in those living in nomadic surroundings and in some country-side village elders of the same position. Probably it was due to his rare modest trait he remained as titular head of the village, as far as Mohammad Hossein, the village oral historian could recollect.

Hassan and family's duration of stay as guests lasted for one long but peaceful month.

Fortunately, January is one of the dry and windy months of the year. In the farming belt region of Somalia, this means rivers are shallow or dry, Mosquito population is temporarily absent or driven away by winds until the next rain fall or river flooding season, it also means harvest time. This enabled Hassan to donate all the anti malaria pills to Warsama's nephew for whom a physician in Mogadishu prescribed them shortly before the breakup of hostilities. It also made it possible for him to witness the harvest process.

Farming in villages relatively distant from the river is mostly dependant on rainfall, generally primitive and use traditional means and tools for cultivation.

This means oxen drawn farming with age old cultivation tools such as axe like implements with a short wooden handle to break ground or for planting seeds. Its function is fairly similar to that of a sickle, in the southern farming belt called as "Yaambo". They also use "Baangad", a machete like big knife to remove thin bush or cut thick weeds.

It is essentially subsistence farming which provide grain as the main staple of food for the farming belt and neighboring regions of southern Somalia. Any extra income eked out of the yearly harvest barely covers other basic family needs.

Given the year long hard work of the farmers and their families coupled with the total absence of any form of meaningful government support, the area and its inhabitants, in spite of their vital contribution to the local economy, remained neglected since colonial times. Matters even got worse after the advent of independence in 1960.

Candidates for the national assembly showed up during election campaigns with rosy promises of providing through national and international aid new model projects, which will improve both the farming methods and life standards by leaps and will enable them catch up with the advanced agricultural societies of the twentieth century. Nothing materialized of those promises, deepening the mistrust of the farmers of all politicians.

When the Military Junta took the reigns of power in a coup d'etat after the assassination of the last elected President of Somalia late1969, they did not pay attention to the important and urgent programs needed by the farmers; instead they were preoccupied with consolidating their own power and cleaning the house by eliminating rivals and opposition from within.

It was only in the wake of the disastrous draught caused famine of the mid 1970's and with the major assistance of their cold war era patron, the defunct Soviet Union, that they launched a massive attempt to relocate famine stricken nomadic families of the Togdheer pastoral belt in the Lower Shabelle farming region. The so called Crash Program launched then as a model project to resettle those families in farming and fishing villages eventually met with failure. Most of the able bodied and bread earning members of each family somehow managed to travel to Saudi Arabia and the Gulf States through close relatives already living and working there.

The war with Ethiopia also dealt a final blow to the whole idea of providing sustained development for the new settlements. The meager resources originally earmarked for relevant assistance to the resettled communities were quickly siphoned by the war effort to liberate the Somali region of south eastern Ethiopia otherwise famously known as the Ogaden.

Apart from the effort to enthusiastically react to the "Dabadheer" famine, the Military Junta did not contribute to improve the lot of the farmers. Instead it became entirely absorbed in directing the whole nation to wage a border war capitalizing on the sentimental dream of the whole Somali people to liberate their ethnic brothers trapped across the border within the borders of neighboring Ethiopia.

The Military Junta, which by the mid seventies was typically reduced to a one man dictatorship, knew very well that the Somali nation did not possess the means to wage a war against its more populous neighbor, Ethiopia, but Muhammad (or Mohamed) Siad Barre, it was later came to be known, either misread or misinterpreted a hint from President Jimmy Carter of the U.S. conveyed through Dr. Robert Cahill, a U.S. citizen who at the time was a personal physician of Sheikh Zayed al Nahyan, President of the United Arab Emirates, that the U.S. may provide logistical support in the form of providing mobile field hospital units for the Somali West Liberation Front militia.

Since the Marxist leaning regime of Col. Menghistu Haile Mariam recently toppled the major African U.S. ally of Emperor Haile Selassie, which tipped the balance of power in cold war era terms in favor of Leonid Brezhnev's Soviet Union government, the U.S. government was waiting for an opportunity to destabilize the new regime.

The message to Siad Barre was one of several endeavors it was pursuing to bring down the Col. Menghistu regime through a combination of internal upheavals, but did not aim to encourage Siad Barre to wage an all out war against its former ally.

After the Siad Barre regime lost the war which turned out a disaster by all accounts, the logical and sensible next step would have been for it to resign and to return the reigns of power to a democratically elected government. Instead it resorted to oppressive measures and internal self entrenchment.

Goats under acacia

The farmers suffered, like other sectors of the population and probably even worse, as the war effort denied them the few support and development funds available in the budget or funneled through international aid and robbed them of manpower, as young able farm hands were forcibly conscripted to the armed forces during the months preceding the border war campaign.

Somali farmers, as a result of chronic negligence and sometimes outright robbery, developed over the last three decades their own brand of resilience in adapting to adverse circumstances, be it their age old reaction to natural calamities or man made crises. Now they faced the biggest and worst form of human caused disasters. Yet Warsama and his folk, being fatalists, were rather resigned to their fate. They may be ambivalent but not ignorant that disaster is in the offing.

The news of besieged dictator Siad Barre's exit from Villa Somalia⁻ arrived to the village by way of bush telegraph in the early hours of January 26th. Osman Mudei, the energetic and outspoken younger brother of Warsama, brought the news to Hassan along with the daily supply of fresh milk from his farm he dutifully provided free for Hassan's children every other morning.

From the first day of Hassan and family's arrival to the village, Hassan sensed he is not a guest for Warsama only but for almost everybody in the village, especially for the Hassan Osman extended family, all nephews of Khadija's stepmother.

In Adalay alone, they were over forty members, outnumbering any other family in the village. Other members of the family lived in Afgoi and Daafeed and few went to work overseas including Arabia and Europe.

In his early forties Osman has spent some time and worked in the Capital, Mogadishu. Now a settled farmer who runs his own farm with the help of his wife and their teenage son, he is one of the more informed citizens in the village and still maintains contact with friends in both Afgoi and Mogadishu.

By breakfast time, Hassan and Khadija decided after consulting with the other family members to move back to Mogadishu and to make sure, first, of the situation in the Capital during their brief stop at Afgoi.

Hassan informed Warsama of their decision and warmly thanked him. He requested him to convey his profuse thanks and gratitude to all the members of his family and friends in the village who were all helpful in welcoming and hosting Hassan and all the members of his family during their stay in their midst. He expressed with an unforgettable and overwhelming gratitude the warmth and security they were given in a very insecure and trying time.

Hassan also visited several other houses in the village to thank each and every family personally for the part they took in creating this memorable and traditionally superb Somali hospitality.

Warsama was rather cautious. He counseled Hassan to hold on for few days until the security situation improved, cooled down in the Capital. Rumors were rife in the village that young tribal militia rebels plus anarchic elements in the Capital got out of hand and went on the rampage during the last few days prior to Siad Barre's fall, looting private property which got into their way and singling out innocent citizens of specific tribal affiliations as targets of ethnic cleansing. Hassan reassured Warsama he will ascertain the real situation whilst in Afgoi before moving back to the Capital.

Donkey carts in Belet Weyne

It was time to hit the trail again. Hassan and family started the journey back to Afgoi after going through a genuinely emotional farewell befitting the occasion. In a way, Hassan considered himself and his family exceptionally fortunate. Throughout their stay in Adalay, Mogadishu residents witnessed the fiercest battle and destruction of a lifetime. All the more so as both Siad Barre and the leadership of the militia played the tribal card, either due to pure wickedness or lack of vision or both.

Many lives could have been saved, had the anti Siad Barre forces initiated and forged a united national front in place well before launching the major offensive on the Capital. Instead, clan rivalries were apparent already in Ethiopia where all the fronts opposed to the Siad Barre regime were divided on tribal and even sub-clan lines.

For example, the Somali National Movement (SNM) who exclusively and single-handedly fought in the northwest of the country for almost a decade and have taken the brunt of all types of persecution and torture in the hands of Siad Barre's regime, including ground and aerial bombardment of Hargeisa and Bur'ao, were already disenchanted with the southern clan based fronts and saw them all equal in considering the north as a perpetual second fiddle to the larger south.

In addition, their political leadership decided, at a certain juncture along their struggle against the Siad Barre regime to exclude all the non-Isaac tribes in the Northwest or what was known in colonial days as British Somaliland Protectorate.

If one really digs into the origin of political and armed dissent and resistance to the Military Junta of Siad Barre, he will find at the beginning there have been genuine attempts to form a broad based national front early in the 1970's.

The Somali Democratic Front (SODF) was founded by prominent Somali personalities representing most Somali clans; but their attempts to make an effective political thrust against the Siad Barre regime came across insurmountable difficulties, partly because of the Ethiopian intelligence quest for Somali Military cadres who can execute armed insurrections to counterbalance the Western Somali Liberation Front's (WSLF) armed incursions into the Ogaden region.

When some high ranking disgruntled Military officers began crossing the border to Ethiopia, the Ethiopian intelligence welcomed them with opened hands and the real business of implementing their grand design of creating fragmented units of clandestine militias to foment chaos across the border with Somalia has finally materialized.

The subsequent influx of dissenting political heavyweights including cabinet members and ambassadors during the 1980's complemented the buildup of several clan based opposition fronts in exile. Ethiopia never had it so good. It had long sought hard to crack the nut of Somali national unity to no avail. Now it found Somali opposition arriving voluntarily at its door step by the dozen.

This dramatic turn of events did not occur because of the concerted covert efforts of the Ethiopian Intelligence Corps, it did occur as a natural consequence of the harsh and repressive practices of the Siad Barre dictatorship directed at any clan considered at odds with the regime.

Refugee camp near Hargeisa 1984

The war with Ethiopia, although initially capitalized on the enthusiastic national fervor of the Somali people and the commendable efficiency of the Military machine, was, nevertheless, a gross political miscalculation.

International strategic experts knew the Somali economy was not in a position to sustain a prolonged full scale war and forecast Somalis will be forced to withdraw within or after seven months back to the current internationally recognized border.

The Soviet Union under Brezhnev, taking an advantage over the U.S. in its cold war era efforts to expand its influence in Africa, has made the strategic choice of supporting its newly prized ally in Africa, namely Marxist leaning Col. Menghistu's Ethiopia over Siad Barre's Somalia and deployed Warsaw Pact expertise in the person of General Petrov and seasoned Cuban troops, probably with prior African field experience in Angola, in time to tip the balance and force the Somali army to vacate gained territory within the disputed borders and withdraw back to the current de facto Somali-Ethiopian border.

In April, 1978, the first real attempt to overthrow Siad Barre occurred. It failed because of betrayal from within the army. Its failure could also be attributed to the fact its core initiators were dominated by a group of Military officers from the Mijertein subclan of the Darod. It was organized and headed by Col. Abdullahi Yusuf who commanded the Bay Military zone at the time.

The failure of this attempted putsch prompted an exodus of high ranking and experienced officers including Col. Yusuf himself. The arrival of Col. Yusuf into Ethiopia made him a prized catch of the Ethiopian intelligence who encouraged him to begin armed insurrections against the Siad Barre regime. Hungry to produce tangible results, the Ethiopians furnished him with the necessary equipment and materiel to conduct his insurgency with swiftness commensurate with their desire.

Military officers from other clans, conscious as they were not to follow another "Darod" Military commander, did participate at first in welcoming Col. Yusuf, but were soon to discover he might be even potentially more dangerous to work with than the dictator whom they fled and were ready and hoping to eventually overthrow.

The officers were discouraged by the mistrust shown by the Colonel who obviously preferred to work only with the officers tribally closest to him. This attitude in itself and the fact he was made the titular head of the SSDF were significant in accelerating the final breakdown of a united national front in exile and compounded the already prevalent cracks amongst the Somali political circles in the exile fed mostly by irate Military officers and grieving civil servants fleeing the injustices of the Siad Barre regime back home.

The emergence of rival clan based fronts in the form of SNM and the USC, representing the Isaac and Hawiye clans respectively, was the inevitable outcome.

The basis for an eventual destruction of a united Somalia has been laid down. A collusion of opposing interests combined to subvert the foundations of the only voluntarily United Nation in this part of the world.

In a way it exposes the disastrous miscalculation of both, the opposition and the ruling Military Junta in either wresting the reigns of power or of holding on, desperately, to it.

The only beneficiary was the Ethiopian regime of Col. Menghistu Haile Mariam which was almost simultaneously deposed after the fall of his erstwhile foe Siad Barre.

Hassan and family arrived back in Afgoi around 2 p.m. accompanied by Warsama's elder son Sheikh Noor. They settled at Hawo Moallim's house again for a brief transit to make sure whether conditions in Mogadishu will permit them to reach their abode in one piece.

After spending the night in Afgoi, Hassan's sister in law, Zeinab suddenly showed up early the next morning of January 27th. She furnished the traveling group with all the vital information they needed.

(On January 28th Radio Mogadishu also announced the formation of a new Interim President in the person of Ali Mahdi Mohammed, chosen by the hitherto secret Central Committee of the USC of which he was the chairman. All the members were of the Hawiye clan and most of them were from the business community in the Capital).

At this point, Hassan headed toward the main Afgoi bus station which he found abuzz with activity. Mini-van buses, mostly Japanese made, with a few Mercedes-Benz vans, were shuttling from Afgoi to Mogadishu and vice versa at the exorbitant fare of So.Sh. 6.000 per passenger.

Hassan booked enough seats for the family including his visiting sister-in-law. Relatives in Mogadishu arranged for the family car to pick up Hassan and the family in two or three trips from the main bus station of Ceel Gaab. Hawo and six of the children boarded the first bus where they were picked by the family car and swiftly taken home to their grand mother who, for the whole difficult and perilous phase, was holding the fort and successfully fended off all sorts of vandals and looters with the help of valiant neighbors and relatives and prevented them from lifting even a spoon from all the three houses as the old lady later said.

Bus stop and market in Mogadishu

Two brothers in law also took part in this effort. They were fortunate, as most of the neighborhood dwellings were either demolished by mortar shells with numerous casualties or were looted of valuable property.

In Hassan's family case no deaths, injuries or damage were incurred. Hassan, Khadija, their infant daughter Amira and his visiting sister in law Zeinab arrived in a subsequent bus. The family car was waiting at the station for the planned immediate transfer.

Khadija's step mother whose idea was to stay at Adalay village whilst the civil war was raging on in the Capital opted to remain in the village for another month.

As soon as the mini-van reached Km 12, it was stopped at the first checkpoint by a group of militia youngsters signaling the change of order in Mogadishu. After one of the group boarded the bus and asked the passengers if members of a certain clan were on board, one or two persons replied with a loud "No". He disembarked and the bus moved on.

Hassan was sitting by the window on the left side of the returning bus. He noticed the Murri (Italian contractor) hangar's corrugated roof being openly stripped by looters. The recently built Ministry of Water and Mineral Resources' and the Highway Development Department's concrete office buildings' windows were also being stripped. Groups of armed civilians instead of uniformed Police or Military personnel suddenly became the norm reflecting the new reality and warning of what is in store for this poor and leaderless nation.

Hassan's spirit sank to its lowest ebb as the stark reality struck home. Despite the apparent calm and the vibrant mood on the waves by Radio Mogadishu, which began playing national songs and music, followed by announcements of the appointment of a new broad based government formed by the newly named President and endorsed by a self appointed committee, originally formed in the waning days of the Siad Barre regime by a group of a broad based veteran politicians mostly from southern clans, the most influential three members of which Ismail Jumale, Haji Muse Boqor and Hashi Weheliye, either died earlier of natural causes or were victims of the violence in the Capital during the January battles to oust Siad Barre.

An abhorrent campaign of clan based man hunt directed at the Darod was being carried out, notwithstanding the continued broadcasts over Radio Mogadishu exhorting the populace not to turn against each other since the major battle against the Dictator is over.

Unfortunately, neither the newly appointed Interim President nor his cabinet, headed by the veteran diplomat and Foreign Minister Omar Arte Ghalib were fully accepted across the country.

Nevertheless, Mr. Ghalib, for reasons only known to himself, hastily issued an order to the armed forces in the northwestern region of the country to hand over their weapons to the SNM militia there. The SNM who, automatically, moved in to fill the vacuum after the Siad Barre forces disbanded or fled in disarray, were not swayed by his order. They continued to consolidate their hold on all the major towns in the northern region.

The SNM leadership did not hide their intention to secede from the south and behaved likewise. From the beginning of the insurgency they declared their main objective was to create a separate state within the confines of the colonial era British Somaliland Protectorate. Those leaders assumed that only the Isaac clan mattered in this campaign.

Other clans within the territorial boundaries of the former British Protectorate could not be either trusted (in the case of the Dolbahante and Warsangeli because of their links to the ruling Marehan clan by lineage to the Darod), because of their traditional political alliance with the Darod (in the case of the Gadabursi) or because they look toward neighboring Djibouti for political inspiration where their Issa cousins held the reign of power since its independence from French rule (in the case of the Issa clan in Zeila).

Few leading intellectuals, notably two prominent lawyers, Yusuf Jama Ali Dhuhul and Mahmoud Ahmed Wali Sheikh Muse, refused to join the SNM, rejecting the tribal exclusivity itself as a destructive and a short sighted dogma.

The underlying strategy of the SNM leadership was to confront the non-Isaac clans with a fait accompli and put them in a situation where they must choose between a culturally closer democratic north or an overwhelmingly domineering, culturally remote south or so they envisaged.

What those leaders failed to take into account was that the essence of the present Somali predicament is the clan based thinking in itself. We have heard many theories and attempts to rationalize tribal based movements. All of them were only contributing to further weakening the only achievement Somalia had made since 1960, which is essentially unity and independence and a modern state aspiring to become a western style designed modern nation.

Admittedly from day one, elected administrations failed to come up with viable solutions to develop or improve on the adequately representative national but locally colonial administrative set up.

Whilst the national system was enshrined in an ideal, sophisticated western representative system which was copied in major part from the Italian constitution, the local government consisted of an inherited colonial system which enabled the central government to conduct local administration through provincial and district commissioners, whilst local government councils including mayoral seats were created through municipal elections, as specified in the adopted national constitution.

Their authority to truly and independently administer municipal and local government matters, however, was undermined by the continued presence of the colonial era centrally controlled Police and civil servants whose daily management of most aspects of public affairs from issuing passports to keeping public security overshadowed the very existence of the municipal authority.

This confusing state of affairs prevailed during the whole nine years of civil administration rule with no significant improvement. When the Military took over power late in 1969, they confused matters further by appointing the provincial Military commander as an ad hoc ruler over all civilian institutions inherited from former administrations. This hastily concocted outfit of a new government in Mogadishu was a gross misconception and a short sighted opportunistic miscalculation of the reality on the ground and was one of the major causes for the ouster of the Siad Barre regime.

The country, after a prolonged period of internal civil war of attrition between an oppressive Military dictatorship and opposing clan based militias that ended in a climatic battle in the Capital, needed a leadership capable of carefully harnessing the dire need for a national healing of the grave wounds inflicted by years of conflict and bloodshed.

Unfortunately, all the protagonists at the forefront of the political spectrum who were supposed to take the initiative of guiding the nation through a genuine healing process did not live up to the task. Some of them turned out to be the very ones who were secretly or openly instigating the massacres taking place around the Capital and in other towns and villages across the country.

The tragedy of the Somali people was starkly manifested in the fact that, after four decades of independence no alternative avenues of political compromise have been explored on a national basis. No real political dialogue did develop amongst the younger educated generations on a national basis at any time since 1960.

The fledgling opposition movements which should have formed

the basis for a true intellectually oriented class were initially hijacked by a combination of opportunist pseudo-clannish tribalists and suppressed by the so called democratically elected governments who could tolerate no free press, public demonstrations nor opposition parties, capable of disturbing the fragile tribal equilibrium which flourished underneath the umbrella of the Somali Youth League (SYL), the reputed political organization which led the struggle for national independence especially in the Italian ruled south.

By the latter half of 1969 and after the infamous electoral fiasco and the assassination of the last democratically elected President, the Somali public had enough of corrupt and inept civilian administrations. The Military found and utilized this heightened sense of public discontent to launch, uninvited but unopposed, its ominous coup d'ètat.

Countryside village

After Hassan and family settled back at home, the family decided he had to be transferred to a friend's house as a precaution. Yet only one week later, his close friend Daahir Ali Daamey, owner of the Daamey Hotel, visited him at the friends' house. They both drove back to Hassan's home.

Not only that. Daahir also volunteered to fetch Hassan's passport from Adalay where, accompanied by Hassan's brother-in-law Sa'di, he drove, approx. 42 km, and back. This timely effort enabled Hassan to travel by air to Rome via Djibouti, thanks to Abdullahi Ahmed Shire, another friend and ex-boss from Hassan's days as a Somali Airlines executive, who told Hassan he only needed to have his passport on the ready as he is arranging to include him as his advisor on aviation matters in an imminent trip he is planning to Italy within one week.

Mr. Shire, (may his soul rest in peace, he died later of natural causes in Mogadishu) was appointed Minister of Transport in the ill fated ad-hoc cabinet of Ali Mahdi and Omer Arte. It is in this capacity he invited his friend Hassan and included him as his aviation consultant for his trip to Italy.

Before departing to Italy on March 1st, 1991, Hassan was visited at home by many friends, among them Major Abdurrahman Jama, who had to walk nearly four kilometers in what has turned out to be dangerous lawless territory since the fall of the Siad Barre regime. With no effective government in place as yet to fill the void, the Capital and the country as a whole suddenly found themselves in total chaos.

The USC or the Hawiye clan based political movement which led the violent but successful assault on the Capital was apparently in agreement on the overthrow of the Siad Barre regime or, as was discovered, during the initial stages of the battle itself, of driving out all of those who ethnically belonged to the Darod clan.

They were not in agreement, however, on how to share power after the Barre regime and the Darod clan are done with. At the heels of the decisive battle for the Capital, political rivalries on a sub-clan level between the two major sub-clans of the Hawiye, namely the Abgaal and the Habar Gidir, each vying for leading the post Siad Barre order in Somalia as it emerged. It was either due to the absence of prior political planning or because of separate sub-clan political ambitions or both.

It was spearheaded by two disparate wings of the clannish political spectrum, namely General Mohamed Farah Aideed and Mr. Ali Mahdi Mohamed.

Ali Mahdi, a Mogadishu businessman of the Abgaal sub-clan who owned a newly opened hotel in Via Mecca and an automotive parts outlet in Ceel Gaab at the center of Mogadishu, was also an active member of the USC central committee in Mogadishu, which was mostly comprised of prominent and nouveau riche businessmen in Mogadishu.

Once the USC central committee hastily chose him to fill the vacuum of country leadership after the ouster of Siad Barre, he wasted no time in engaging in daily presidential activity from appointing a Prime Minister and his cabinet to filling high level civil service positions, drawing early criticism.

On the wings with his core Habar Gidir clan fighters stationed in Balad on the northern outskirts of Mogadishu was General Aideed who, only few days after Ali Mahdi's assumption of the presidency was announced, voiced his opposition to Mr. Mahdi's appointment as unacceptable and declared in no uncertain terms his own ambition for the post. He also declared himself as the legitimate chairman of the USC and the commander in chief of the USC militia forces. This was seen by the various sub-clans as an ominous sign of divisiveness amongst the hitherto united ranks of the Hawiye clan.

Energetic goodwill efforts by clan elders resulted in a USC congress held in Hiran to elect a new chairman for the USC. The candidate rivaling Aideed for the chairmanship was Ali Haji Yusuf, a prominent educator who ran a successful middle level private school establishment in Wardhiigley district before getting involved in USC political movement.

Aideed won the chairmanship but still continued his quest for the presidency. Some of his militia who wore the same uniform as Siad Barre's Presidential Guard symbolically occupied Villa Somalia, signaling to every one that only Aideed could reside there.

Meanwhile Siad Barre, who was forced out of the Capital by the USC militias was still in the southern port of Kismayo with what remained of his army and a lot of dislocated Darod refugees. The threat of an attempted comeback by Siad Barre, although a remote possibility, was still there.

After a failed attack attempted by the Ali Mahdi troops to drive Siad forces from Kismayo, Aideed took charge of another attempt and succeeded in pushing Siad Barre out of the important port city of Kismayo to his home town of Garbaharey.

Militia fighter

Aideed's political stock amongst the Hawiye USC supporters rocketed to unparalleled heights. It also brought him closer to a collision course with Ali Mahdi's government and to his Mudulood supporters. Mudullood being a group of sub-clans, composed of Abgaal, Ojaajeen, Wacdaan, Hiillibey and Mobleen. They are all tribal brothers and cousins but the Abgaal form the majority amongst them.

From his newly confirmed position as Chairman of the USC Aideed issued several proposals on how and which policies should be adopted by Ali Mahdi and his government.

When Ali Mahdi rejected these proposals with the implicit suggestion that the party should be confined to its role, political confrontation began. Aideed declared himself as the legitimate President of Somalia.

From there on, a political tug of war began accompanied by unnecessary show of force by both sides. General Aideed then launched an all out attack on Ali Mahdi's camp in November 1991, which developed rapport into an ugly, divisive and violent war thwarting any conceived hope of finding a solution to the Somali quagmire.

The worst part of the whole affair was, whilst the leaders of the USC were engaged in their own localized conflict, the whole nation lay in tatters and was crying for a unifying leader or personality in possession of a national appeal and with a vision beyond tribal skirmishes.

It didn't matter if this leader was from Mogadishu or Hargeisa. Unfortunately, none of the protagonists at the forefront of the competing political forces lived up to these desperately needed qualities to lead a nation diving into abysmal chaos.

While Ali Mahdi and Aideed were driving the two major sub-clans into a renewed civil war, further exacerbating the already disastrous state of affairs, prompting the international community to intervene, the SNM in the north were pursuing their own goal of unilateral secession, thereby creating a new dimension to an already intractable and internationally unprecedented conflict.

Many foreign observers remarked Somalia may be the first casualty of the vacuum, created by the post cold war international order where spheres of influence are no longer contested by two major super powers or their affiliates.

The Secretary General of the United Nations (UN), then Dr. Boutros Ghali, took the initiative of focusing world attention on Somalia when he criticized the economically advanced nations for ignoring African problems whilst being preoccupied with the Balkans.

As a result an American led, United Nations sponsored, humanitarian effort named "Operation Restore Hope" was launched. The idea behind this international rescue operation was to ensure emergency food supplies to the areas worst hit by the deadly combination of famine and civil war in the country, get into the hands of the deserving and needy and prevent it from being waylaid or high jacked by tribal militias who thus far have confiscated already available grain stocks in the country by force.

This well intentioned effort was hampered by two sad and tragic factors. It seems that some of the United Nations Organization's campaigns have met with more failures than successes during the 1960's since it replaced the defunct League of Nations after World War II.

Its envoy to Palestine Count Bernadotte was assassinated during the first Arab Israeli conflict. A crisis that remains a chronic destabilizing factor in one of the most volatile regions in the world. Its famous Secretary General, Dag Hammerskjold, died in a mysterious air-crash in Katanga during the Congo crisis in 1960.

After decades of authoritarian rule under Mobutu Sese Seko, another civil war is currently raging in that country again throughout which he was ousted. His successor President Cabila was also assassinated and ousted. Cabila's son inherited the rule, but the war is still raging on.

Ironically Somalia was, until this ill fated "Operation Restore Hope" one of the successes in the Organization's history. The UN General Assembly voted in 1949 to put the southern part of Somalia under a UN Trusteeship administered by Italy and supervised by three members, Colombia, Egypt and the Philippines, for a period of ten years with a mandate to grant the territory full independence at the expiry of this period. This was successfully accomplished.

Somalia's fully independent nation was born on July 1st, 1960. In a unique celebration of both union and independence, the southern part, which for a decade was under the trusteeship of the UN, merged with the northern part or the British Protectorate of Somaliland which was declared independent on June 26th, 1960, uniting the first two parts of five Somali inhabited territory divided by European powers into five separate parts, when they carved the African continent into colonized properties at their Berlin boundary conference of 1885.

There is no doubt the initial reaction of the world community and of the United States government under President George H. Bush to the horrors, caused by the combined misery of war and famine, was timely and called for.

The success of forming the international coalition also bears witness to President Bush administration's sure footed ability to mobilize the international community for a humanitarian cause following the footsteps of the successful Gulf war campaign. Things turned sour, however, after the diverse United Nations forces arrived on the ground in Somalia.

Apart from the intricate procedural and bureaucratic maze of determining or assigning logistical responsibilities, the biggest hurdle, it turned out, was in leadership and policy. It became immediately apparent the US was constrained by its own laws not to allow its armed forces to operate under the command of a foreign military organization albeit a UN humanitarian rescue mission.

The Europeans also appeared to have a different approach (in the case of France) on how to deal with disarming the rival Somali militias to neutralize them as a means of realizing peace. They immediately began to collect arms in a house to house search operation.

Local militias who were initially stunned by the magnitude of international reaction to Operation Restore Hope and the massive arrival of "United Task Force" (UNITAF) troops had no choice but to cooperate, given the popular welcome these forces received in the Capital.

The U.S. government, however, saw otherwise and began implementing a policy of negotiating with the leadership of the stronger militia forces by posting Ambassador Robert Oakley, a career diplomat, who already served in Somalia as an ambassador in the early 1980's and was later appointed head of the anti-terrorism office in the State Department, as a special envoy to particularly engage the belligerent militia leader General Aideed in peaceful negotiations and to convince him of the real humanitarian intention of Operation Restore Hope.

The American policy, despite some limited initial coaxing of Aideed and other faction leaders to dump heavy weapons, was short lived and backfired on two fronts. On the one hand, some European governments who eagerly participated in the UNITAF effort, namely France and Italy, were critical of what they saw as the US government's single handed approach of an international rescue effort to which they committed their own military personnel and also of the U.S. administration's insistence of commanding all forces arriving Mogadishu albeit under a UN arrangement.

Not only that, France quickly decided to withdraw its contingent from the Capital within few weeks and only after demonstrating to the Somali residents of Mogadishu how different their style was from the American's. Many Somalis in Mogadishu and abroad agreed with the French, prompting the UN to change the intervention forces name to "United Nations Operations in Somalia" (UNOSOM) and to expand the mission's objective to combat those militias who forcibly attempt to stop relief supplies from reaching mine infested destinations.

The UN also appointed a new military command headed by Admiral Jonathan Howe, a retired U.S. Navy Vice Admiral. The intervention force entered another phase when the UN Security Council authorized its forces on the ground to enter into combat under chapter VII of the UN charter in March, 1993 if their rescue missions were hindered by local militias, and have set a precedent which observers thought was called for at the time but eventually entangled the organization in endless problems.

Italy lingered on for a while. Their attempts to convince the Somali public of a more friendly approach and to meddle in local Somali politics by courting old colonial time friends like the now deceased General Mohamed Ibrahim Ahmed "Liiq liiqato", who, at the time, was an influential elder of the USC ended with mediocre results. It also lead to rumors among the Somalis, the Italians were the source of strategic leakages of the UNOSOM planned operations to Aideed's militia.

This kind of wrangling over who should lead the intervention forces served only to demonstrate a lack of clear vision of how to execute a well intentioned humanitarian rescue operation. It also indicated how difficult it is for the UN to manage diverse armed contingents and direct them to perform in harmony in adverse circumstances.

All told, it contributed to the degeneration of the whole effort into a narrowly focused one man hunt with an anticlimactically disastrous ending.

Hassan boarded the Somali Airlines Dornier aircraft that was to take him with Mr. Shire and two other delegates via Djibouti. The entry visas to Italy were to be obtained from the Italian Consulate in Djibouti.

Before leaving home to the airport, Hassan was slightly apprehensive about the uncertain atmosphere engulfing the Airport area. Incidents of ethnic profiling were a daily occurrence, given the absence of a law enforcement authority replacing the toppled regime's Police.

Militias who participated in the battle for Mogadishu remained there as temporary custodians until a new authority emerged. These militias were loyal only to their own commanders. Fortunately for Hassan they were from Mr. Shire's region of Hiran. In addition, some of Hassan's ex-colleagues of Somali Airlines were still handling flights.

Mogadishu Km 4 and airport

As Hassan arrived at the airport entrance, Ahmed Jama, the Station Manager welcomed him with a jovial smile and wished him a happy trip. When one of the militias asked about the identity of the passenger, Ali Ulusow, a civil aviation department officer, told him Hassan is a member of the Minister of Transport's delegation.

After spending some time chatting with few other friends including Abdulle Ashur, a flight engineer, Yusuf Jama Barre and Ali Roble Geedi, both members of the airport Somali Airlines' station staff, Hassan remained for twenty minutes by the Dornier aircraft earmarked for the flight.

With him was Mohamed Gure, a faithful ex colleague who insisted to be on Hassan's side lest any of the trigger happy militias commit an unexpected act which may harm him or his friends. Gure also happened to be from the same region.

Things were so much out of control that a supporter of the USC confided to Hassan his worries of a very dark future awaiting the residents of Mogadishu and also of his own plans to leave the ongoing mess to a safer place.

Mr. Shire and the other passengers arrived meanwhile. Few minutes later the flight took off to Djibouti.

On the flight to Djibouti many contradictory thoughts preoccupied Hassan. On the one hand he was thankful to God that, after all of what happened, his own family were in one piece and back at their home. His sister and half-brother were also still alive in their home. Except for his former step father who was murdered by a tribal militia in the aftermath of the Mogadishu battle, everybody else in the family was safe.

On the other hand, Hassan was worried of what might happen next in the fluid political situation and the anarchic atmosphere hovering over the Capital and the rest of the country. Nobody appeared to be in control. From conversations of the few passengers on the flight, it was clear everybody was apprehensive of what is going to happen next. Things went so much out of hand, no one could envisage what local force or authority shall be capable of persuading the militias to return their weapons.

Although no significant dissent surfaced at this early stage within the ranks of the USC, since Siad Barre and the remnants of his forces were still regrouping in Kismayo, posing a threat he might stage a come back, yet rumors that Aideed and some of the militia commanders coming from rural areas were not satisfied with the all civilian cabinet formed by USC central committee which was mostly composed of prominent Mogadishu businessmen, were already rife in the Capital.

It prompted Hassan to recall a pamphlet published by Egal, the last civil Prime Minister in the pre-Siad Barre era, also the now deceased President of the breakaway northwestern region of Somaliland, in the waning days of Siad Barre's regime in 1990 during a spate of manifestos (Bayaans) that flooded Mogadishu, in which he proposed that Siad Barre steps aside in favor of his deputy Gen. Hussein Kulmiye Afrah and an ex Prime Minister from the northwest region, probably Mohamed Hawadleh Madar, prior to convening a national conference of reconciliation.

More important was his warning, unless the militias engaged in combating the Barre regime in the regions are represented in this conference, the country runs the risk of civil war since these militias will never accept former politicians to benefit from the fruits of their bloody struggle. Subsequent events proved what Egal predicted in his manifesto to be correct up to a certain point.

The flight landed at Djibouti International Airport on approximately 11.00 a.m. interrupting Hassan's train of reminiscences. Mr. Shire, Hassan and the other two passengers on a different mission to Italy were whisked to the Sheraton Hotel where they stayed whilst their visas to Italy were being arranged.

The delegation boarded an Air France flight on the second week of March 1991 to Roma via Paris. They stayed in the Ciceroni Hotel which was the usual place for Somali Airlines executives since the 1970's.

Two Presidents, Abdullahi Salad, who actually presided over the Airline while Siad Barre's government reigned and Mohamed Siad Barre's last appointee, and Mohamoud Guleed, whom Ali Mahdi appointed in a hurry without even consulting his own Minister of Transport, turned up in Rome each claiming to be the legitimate head of the national flag carrier.

The Italian authorities, having no stomach to be drawn into the fallout of Somalia's civil war, referred their dispute to relevant civil judicial process. Apparently, Ali Mahdi, lacking experience and under political pressure from his own sub-clan, issued several high level administrative appointments to fill posts vacated by the ousted regime. This was done in such a haste, however, no consideration of public sensitivities or legal implications were taken into account.

The ad-hoc government itself was still under a question mark. Neither the international community nor the local political situation were ready to digest any business as usual dealings with anyone in Somalia until matters come into a better light. National and international reactions depended on how the still volatile and explosive situation will develop.

Although Siad Barre was ousted from the Capital, he set camp in Kismayo with his supporters planning his next step. In Mogadishu, Aideed began grumbling for not being considered for the presidential post. In fact his militia took over Villa Somalia (the Presidential Palace) to prevent any other occupant from entering.

No semblance of authority remained in the regions. Militias were roaming the country causing havoc and inflicting mayhem all over. In such a situation where matters hung in an extremely delicate balance, it was next to impossible for anybody to take a stand, but Somalia was perilously sinking into abysmal chaos at enormous speed.

After the Minister learned of the complicated legal aspects shrouding the whole Somali situation, he decided to stay in Rome longer than he anticipated. Hassan then asked permission to proceed to Germany to finalize pending matters with Lufthansa which he represented in Somalia for the last seven years.

After getting in touch by phone with friends at German Cargo, the subsidiary freight carrier of Lufthansa that operated forth nightly flights to Mogadishu up to one week before the flare up of hostilities. In Frankfurt, they were happy to hear from their agent in Mogadishu and immediately requested the German consulate in Rome to facilitate entry visa. They also arranged free local transport on a Lufthansa flight within few days.

Hassan was in Frankfurt as planned. The operations manager Wolfgang Duffner and sales manager David Keary were as welcoming and sympathetic as usual. They informed Hassan of how they were overwhelmed by urgent phone calls from all his German friends. True friends like Herbert and Bärbel Warnke who were very much worried about his safety and the well being of his family.

They also passed on an open invitation to visit them in their home at Troisdorf near Bonn or at Westerland on Sylt Island, where Herbert was undergoing therapeutic treatment for respiratory allergic complications, and offered to get him there on a Lufthansa domestic flight.

Hassan obliged himself by making a phone call to thank his friends for their concern. He informed them he accepted their invitation and opted to go to Westerland first and check his convalescing friend's health soon after he finishes business with Lufthansa.

His friends at Lufthansa also arranged for his entry visa to be extended for three months. This gave him enough time to visit with friends and to plot the future destination for his family.

Although the Warnkes made him feel at home, his urgent priority was to return to Mogadishu and find the safest way to get his family out and in the meantime work, while he is in Europe, to arrange the necessary travel documents for them. Before leaving Mogadishu he took care of taking enough passport size photos for the same purpose.

To Hassan's dismay, however, international flights immediately stopped using Mogadishu airport for obvious safety reasons. For some time, no one could travel to and out of the Capital except delegations from the USC's declared ad-hoc Cabinet Ministers, newly named civil servants and few individuals or families fortunate enough to get booked on the Somali Airlines Dornier flights still serving the Mogadishu-Djibouti route.

This meant chances of ferreting out Hassan's family were dim indeed. After being stranded for two months in Germany amongst German and Somali friends, during which Hassan spent a wonderful time with the Warnkes and Mohamed Moallim, the Frankfurt District Manager of Somali Airlines, who insisted Hassan should remain his guest while in Frankfurt and through whom Hassan maintained constant contact with Somali Airlines office in Rome.

When Hassan learned that several people, among them some Somali Airlines officers, were also stranded in Rome and are waiting for the opportunity to fly back to Mogadishu, Hassan set out to move back to Rome and seize the opportunity to get the family out of Mogadishu by which ever means possible.

Arranging travel documents and entry visas to Egypt for Hassan and the whole family was facilitated by two members of the Somali consulate staff in Rome who were related to Hassan by marriage and by Mr. Awes of Somali Airlines' Rome office through the intervention of Somali Airlines Director of Marketing Madina Amir. The happy coincidence that was in store for Hassan though, was when he found himself on the same flight with Madina who was returning to Mogadishu.

When he arrived in Djibouti, Hassan learned the situation in Mogadishu deteriorated further. Anarchy became so rampant, no person in his senses would set foot at Mogadishu airport without personal protection awaiting to shield him from attack. As Hassan did not fit the category who could organize a band of militia or even few bodyguards for that matter, he was halted in his tracks in Djibouti.

Madina, who was still carrying out her Somali Airlines duty, volunteered to pay a visit to his family and to help facilitate their departure on the first possible passenger flight departing Mogadishu airport to Djibouti. She also took important mail to Khadija.

Ten days after Madina arrived in Mogadishu she was able to visit Hassan's house and family, arrange for them to travel on a chartered passenger flight and asked Mahmoud Hassan Salteye to help with their transportation and assistance with departure formalities through the Airport.

Thanks to the valuable and helpful friends and former Somali Airlines colleagues, Khadija and children arrived at Djibouti Airport in one piece on May 4th, 1991.

When he went to the Djibouti Airport officers, seeking information about incoming flights from Mogadishu earlier that morning, they seemed not to be aware of any. Hassan was later told that, because of the uncertain situation in Mogadishu and Somalia as a whole, and after the sudden collapse of regular administrative institutions, they get news of incoming flights only minutes prior to the aircraft entering Djibouti airspace.

By late evening, however, Hassan had the pleasant surprise of reuniting with his loved ones at the reception counter of the Plain de Ciele Hotel in Djibouti where he was temporarily staying at the time.

Abdurrahman Duale, Director General of the Somali Commercial Bank and a long time friend, happened to be leaving Hotel Menelik when a taxi driver approached him to ask if he knew a Mr. Hassan Ali Jama from Mogadishu, whose family just arrived and are looking for him. Abdurrahman smiled, boarded the taxi and guided the family to the Plain de Ciele Hotel. Hassan obligingly thanked his friend.

Hassan's family spent the night at the hotel. The following morning, however, Hassan got in touch with a cousin who already offered to host Khadija and the kids. The cousin, Fadumo Ibrahim, came in person to the hotel and accompanied them to her apartment where they stayed until their flight to Egypt through Sana'a, Yemen, materialized.

Three months after the fall of Siad Barre, another despot, Col. Menghistu Haile Mariam of neighboring Ethiopia, was also ousted. Foreigners leaving Ethiopia, as a result, added more pressure to the already heavy backlog of reserved space on the few flights operating out of Djibouti to Europe and the Middle East.

Hassan's family had to board a Yemenia (Yemen Airways) flight on June 18th, to Sana'a. When they arrived Sana'a, the station staff of Yemenia, apologetically, announced to transiting passengers that due to a one day industrial action (strike) by flight crews all passengers departing their flights are cancelled. Overnight lodging was provided by the carrier at the Hadda Ramada Inn near the airport who also provided transport.

Hassan and Khadija were satisfied with the two rooms and the service at the Hotel, but they also found it is harder to move five children across modern international airports than across local villages on donkey carts.

The harsh equatorial sun, rough dirt and gravel pathways of the Somali hinterland becomes smooth sailing in comparison with the inefficient, sometimes bureaucratic and rigid regulations imposed by immigration authorities.

If and when an industrial action becomes a factor for further delay then one has only to surrender to fate. Early the next morning the whole family returned to the airport ostensibly to board the Cairo bound flight, only to discover the industrial action by Yemenia is still on after negotiations between the flight personnel union and the airline management failed.

In a last desperate attempt for a way out of this seemingly hopeless impasse Hassan remembered that the traffic manager of Yemenia was a class mate of his, in the 1950's, during their younger days in Aden. He sent him a message through the station officer on duty to be kind enough to transfer them under the circumstances onto the Egypt Air flight scheduled to leave one hour later to Cairo.

One hour and a half later to the clock, the happy news came that all transiting passengers heading to Cairo or beyond Cairo may immediately board the Egypt Air departing flight. Hassan and Khadija huddled the kids in line through the relevant gate leading to the waiting modern 767 jet aircraft.

Young Somali boy

Egypt

As Egyptair flight arrived at Cairo International Airport early after-noon on June 19th, 1991, the passengers were driven by aerodrome transport to the second terminal which caters mostly for Middle Eastern and African flights.

Hassan and Khadija braced for a long wait. Delays of all sorts, either due to lack of well advanced airport passenger and baggage dispatch systems or because of tedious immigration and security procedures, are usually expected in this part of the world.

If, on top of that, your passport happens to originate from a hot trouble spot like Somalia, you become a subject of extra judicious scrutiny. You have no room for complaint. Though Hassan and the family's traveling documents were as sound as any normal family would be, Hassan did not wish to give any uncooperative immigra-tion officer a chance to cause the tired family further hardship.

Hassan's main other worry was about the undue suffering which might be caused to his friend Abdulkadir Aden and/or his family who might be outside waiting for their arrival. Hassan met with Ab-dulkadir while he was visiting with his father who was attending the first international attempt to convene a reconciliation conference among the warring Somali factions.

After the fall of Siad Barre a conference was hosted by President Hassan Guled of the Republic of Djibouti and was supported by all major international powers.

Aden Abdulle Osman enjoys a unique position in Somali history, being the first democratically elected President of a unified indepen-dent Somali nation on July 1st, 1960. For this reason, he was chosen to chair the conference.

Two other prominent figures in Somali modern history, namely, Mohamed Ibrahim Egal, who was the first Prime Minister of ex British Somaliland Protectorate when it gained independence from Great Britain and led the northern parts of Somalia to unite with its southern parts, and Abdurazak Haji Hussein who was a noted So-mali Youth League (SYL) activist in the years preceding indepen-dence, when the British Military Administration (BMA) and the Italian Trusteeship Aministrazione Fudiciaria Italo Somalia (AFIS), both tried to suppress the Somali struggle toward unity and independence.

Then he became a Minister of Internal Affairs in the first Somali cabinet after independence and moved on to become Prime Minister of the most nationally acclaimed civilian government in the mid sixties. Now generally considered by most Somalis as the honeymoon period of the Somali modern democratic experience. Both these gentlemen were chosen as vice chairmen.

It was during this time Hassan met with Abdulkadir and informed him of his intention to come with the family to settle in Cairo while in transition. After awaiting the customary time it takes the Cairo Airport immigration officers to process a complete family, Hassan and the family went out to be met by Abdulkadir's wife, Hawo, his son Omer and his sister Fadumo.

They were driven to the Oasis Hotel at Heliopolis, close to where Abdulkadir and many other friends from Mogadishu and their families lived. After being welcomed by Abdulkadir and having lunch together at his apartment, Hassan, accompanied by Fadumo Aden, embarked upon looking for an apartment for his family.

Looking for an apartment in Cairo the local way, however, might be lighter on the budget but it, certainly, is heavier and more taxing on both the feet and the nerves. One has to find the most popular watchman in the neighborhood, who also doubles as a free lance real estate agent relying mostly on first hand knowledge of all vacant apartments in the vicinity and an expert like familiarity of the current rent value of significant available space.

There is also the possibility of the commission he is asking for this brand of real estate brokerage may be unreasonably inflated. It is generally expected that you do not give in easily and dismiss the first offered rate all together. This will lead you to an endless haggling game in which one's wits are pitted against that of the wily but sometimes amiable fellow who has been hardened by years of experience.

In Hassan's case, the famous watchman broker was "Am Saaber" or uncle Sabir, a soft spoken old man from the Aswan province in Upper Egypt. After listening to a detailed account of the current situation of available apartments in the neighborhood, known as "kulliyet el-banat" or girls' college, Hassan decided, instead of going through the tedious process of price haggling, to settle for the first apartment which fits his family's needs and falls within the range of his immediate budgetary constraints.

He was too tired and had no stomach for another night in transition. Within half an hour a tentative deal has been reached with the owners of an apartment only half a block from the Oasis Hotel, with the understanding that Hassan's family may move the following morning after the apartment have been readied for the new occupants.

By afternoon of the next day Khadija and the five children were in the apartment. Hassan was shopping in the neighborhood for provisions and other household needs. However, with the family secure in a rented apartment, Hassan felt he finally found a temporary respite during the schools' early summer vacation period, since he will have to begin late summer the task of facing up to enroll the kids into schools.

This meant going through grueling and tedious red tape even with respect to private schools. Public school education in Egypt is limited to Egyptian nationals only. Arab league member nations' citizens have traditionally enjoyed certain limited exemptions to enroll their children in private schools, though curriculums for all educational institutions are supervised and approved by the Ministry of Education to ensure a unitary standard.

With or without exemptions, red tape remains the same. It has become so endemic in the Egyptian civil service and part of Egypt's urban folklore that humorous anecdotes of the role it plays in the Egyptian citizens' life are featured by the daily press. Cartoons depicting lethargic functionaries torturing the public in government offices with stupid delaying tactics are also part of the pass times for the daily tabloids' readers.

Nevertheless, out of dire necessity, parents have to endure the long lines at the respective regional offices and adjust to the local ways. If you are conversant with the Arabic language and with the Egyptian dialect, in particular, you may eventually conform or adjust to the Egyptian "routine" system, following the famous conformist adage "if you cannot beat them, join them".

Since Cairo offered a perfect safe haven for Hassan and the family, he and Khadija decided it is the most convenient place to stay while matters evolve back home. Compared to the situation in Somalia, any obstacles one may face may be dealt with as part of the normal daily life struggle; besides, as one of the most important Capitals in the Middle East, it has become since the 1980's a vital international center of trade and communications from which you can easily get connected to anywhere.

Any one who visited Cairo in the early 1970's, as Hassan did, will have immediately observed a marked improvement in communication and the services sector in general. Although further improvement is still required, if progress continued at the pace it began in the early '90s, there is no doubt, Cairo will accomplish its target to be in a position commensurate to its importance as an international hub of tourism, trade and communications, unless it is slowed by bureaucratic inertia and the snail paced transition between the old state controlled economy and the haphazardly confusing privatization policies.

Nevertheless, one positive aspect that will not escape the attention of any foreign resident in Cairo is the high level of safety which the local Police have been able to maintain in such a great and densely populated (approx. 15 million inhabitants) metropolis.

Some observers attribute this to the fact that Egypt have for decades been controlled by the armed forces, whether because of internal political power change from monarchy to military dictatorship or due to the volatile politics of the Middle East, which both necessitate maximum vigilance that sometimes borders on paranoia, resulting in undue pressure on the population at times.

However, given the almost impossible circumstances prevalent in an era when internal security forces' efforts were overstretched grappling with issues of rampant terrorism before the west saw the worst of it, any safety conscious resident had only to commend the success of the local Police for achieving and maintaining this high standard of safety.

Hassan managed to enroll the four elder children in a private school only few miles away from the family's residence. Amira, the youngest, one year and seven months old was taken to a neighboring private kindergarten on the same street.

The next step was to find possibilities of engaging in a useful activity while the situation back home evolves, hopefully, to the better. In his last encounter with German Cargo managers, everybody was of the opinion to wait for things to sort themselves out.

The civil war was still going on. Uncontrolled, anarchy reigned after the ouster of Siad Barre. The failure of the numerous clan based militias to come up with a viable alternative led to more devastation and to the disintegration of the country. Somalia was reduced to the level of a "failed state".

The resulting depredation and famine called for international humanitarian intervention. Hence "Operation Restore Hope", spearheaded by the George Bush administration of the U.S.

Still, Mr. Duffner, a man known for his carefully studied opinions, held the optimistic view that Somalia will be back on its feet within two to three years at the most.

Subsequently, Mr. Duffner and Mr. Keary sent a letter to Hassan in Cairo, informing him that, as German Cargo is planning to expand its operations, they will try to make use of his services in the appropriate field.

Meanwhile they promised, subject to approval of higher management, to contribute a certain monthly sum to augment his cost of living in Cairo.

To his surprise Hassan received no further news from them. After waiting for sometime, Hassan learned that the whole subsidiary of German Cargo Services was totally absorbed by its parent company Lufthansa.

It came as another shock to Hassan, who was eagerly awaiting the opportunity of continuing to serve in the career he was known to have practiced for the last two decades, and was aware that this could best be conducted through the people he represented and dealt with in Mogadishu and Frankfurt in the 1980's, throughout which he cultivated reliable personal and professional relationships. Alas, it was not to be.

This meant that he had to contact his childhood friends who decided to seek work and residence in the Persian Gulf area nearly three decades ago as a last resort. He was certain each and every one of them shall spare no effort to help.

Because of the political disequilibrium caused by the Gulf War of 1990, resulting in a drastic shift of emphasis by the rich oil producing states who began some sort of economic retrenchment by shelving most of their development oriented projects, focusing on and strengthening their defense needs. And due to the fact that, after three decades, as life's twists and turns affected everyone's circumstances, it was by no means an easy task to allocate a newcomer into the Gulf area's job market.

Nevertheless, his friend, AbdurRahman Saeed, now an Omani citizen, invited to visit with him at Muscat, where he worked as a personnel manager in one of the branches of an Omani bank. He arranged a three month entry visa and a return air ticket for Hassan's trip. Hassan boarded the Gulf Air flight to Muscat on a mildly hot late summer day at Cairo International Airport. As the flight was making a stop over at Dubai Airport, it was full, almost crowded with Egyptian teachers returning to work toward the end of the summer school vacation.

When the flight finally arrived at Seeb International Airport, in the early evening, it took little time to pass through immigration formalities. AbdurRahman Saeed, accompanied by his eldest son Mohammed, was there to pick him up.

After a five minute drive, they all arrived at AbdurRahman's residence in Ruwi, one of Muscat's suburbs close to the airport. Safia, AbdurRahman's wife, was there to give an excellent sisterly welcome. She knew Hassan from the days when she and her cousin AbdurRahman were newly weds. Hassan took part in their wedding ceremony in 1961 in Aden as a family friend and as a neighbor.

They were neighbors again in Mogadishu when circumstances forced most of the Somali community to return back to their homeland during the mid sixties, as Aden was plunged into turmoil prior to independence and dismantling of the last base of the British forces there.

It was also the second time Hassan visited Muscat in two decades. In 1974, Hassan arrived at Seeb International as a Somali Airlines marketing officer to check how a recently introduced weekly flight was being handled at Seeb Airport and how to explore a growing air travel market between Oman and East Africa was making progress.

He met AbdurRahman at the time when he was a recent arrival

trying to establish himself before the family joined him. Although he did not realize his objective, Hassan spent a splendid time in a family atmosphere and was happy to be introduced to his friends' offspring, some of whom have become married with their own households. Mohammed became a US educated engineer, married and with two lovely children, Faisal, the second son was also married, and his wife delivered their first child, a beautiful daughter, only two days after Hassan's arrival. Mahmoud was away attending training as a communication technician in Doha, Qatar. Rashid was a freshman at the University of Oman. Muna was a high school senior and Khaled 11 years old, the youngest, was in middle school.

In a repeat effort to help Hassan relocate in the Gulf area, AbdurRahman invited him in 1996 to Dubai, where he arranged for him to participate in a commercial venture with a group of Somali businessmen based in the Emirates. Unfortunately, a major partner abruptly withdrew at the last minute citing family reasons.

Nevertheless, Hassan took the opportunity to check with his other childhood friends, including Ismail Jama, Ismail Sheikh and Ahmed Abdi and also to visit with Dr. Abdi Ahmed Farah Pakistan, a nickname he picked up in younger days while still in school. Probably because he resembles folks from Madras as many Somalis do.

Dr. Pakistan, a close friend, extended an open invitation to Hassan on an earlier visit to Cairo to move his family to his work place in Abu Dhabi. During the flare-up of hostilities in Mogadishu, January 1991, it was in his house where Hassan and his family took a safe shelter before fleeing the perilous battle ground of Mogadishu to the nearby countryside. This time, he insisted that he be Hassan's host although there were other invitations awaiting him in Abu Dhabi.

Hassan decided to honor his friend by apologizing to his childhood friend, Ismail Jama. When Hassan arrived at the taxi station in Abu Dhabi, Dr. Pakistan was there to take him home, where he spent nine days in a family atmosphere. His wife, Marian, was a superb hostess and the children, Farah, Ruqiya and Ijabo, were simply lovable.

Hassan was inundated by invitations from his childhood friends and from relatives. Hardly one day passed-by without being at a friend's or a kin's house. Except during working hours which he reserved for attempted job seeking or business contacts, his evenings were mostly booked by childhood pals.

Most enjoyable evening was spent with Ahmed Abdi, since deceased, when, after dinner, they had a long walk along the clean and modern pavements of Abu Dhabi, exchanging nostalgic youth memories and present day realities, including but not limited to the catastrophic events engulfing the common homeland.

Mohamed Elmi Salah was leaving to participate in a work related seminar in London, Great Britain, the same day Hassan arrived to Dubai. He was a naturalized United Arab Emirates (UAE) citizen for at least a decade. He promised to try his best level to search for a suitable work position befitting Hassan's career, although he intimated few months later his efforts did not yield positive results. Hassan was thankful nevertheless.

By the end of the year 1995, the family savings were getting depleted, hopes of landing a job anywhere diminished and Somalia was sinking deeper into crises after both the UN and the United States Forces withdrew from there, inspiring the international community to leave that hapless and failed state nation to its own devices.

Hassan pondered for a while what to do next. On the one hand he had seven mouths to feed including his mother in law in an expensive foreign environment, on the other, his last attempts to find employment to support them vanished into thin air.

One week after he returned to Cairo, he met with his friend Dr. Osman Aden, who recently came to Cairo to spend time with his family also residing in a neighboring street. Dr. Osman, a prominent Somali physician, proposed to initiate a pharmaceutical import company in Mogadishu as a way of providing beneficial and affordable service to the suffering population who are in dire need of medicines, especially because the chaotic and endemically hostile environment in Somalia, where even care givers who volunteered to help the needy were often victims of random kidnapping and murder by thugs who are holding the whole nation as hostage in collusion with their warlord masters.

The idea sounded logically excellent from a patriotic and humanitarian aspect; its viability from a pure business viewpoint looked less attractive. Hassan worried much about the safety of Dr. Osman himself. Matters in Mogadishu reached their lowest ebb in the 1990's, especially after the departure of UNOSOM forces, and the Somali crisis was shelved as a hopeless case.

Nevertheless, Hassan decided to accept the proposal and embarked on launching the pharmaceutical venture with his friend. The first shipment was sent by air via Djibouti to one of the militia controlled airports on the northern fringes of Mogadishu.

Dr. Osman made an excellent job of arranging with the private operators of the Cessna flights on the Mogadishu-Djibouti sector for efficient and smooth transshipment of the imports to their final destination.

Minor difficulties were encountered at first, but against all odds and, in part, due to the persistence of all participants in the venture, shipments continued successfully through the Djibouti route until they grew both in volume and size that it became necessary to look for alternative means of transport.

After a careful research of the best possible route, it was decided to use the Kenyan port of Mombasa which was already being used by the energetic Somali merchants who kept the Mogadishu inhabitants supplied with all sorts of goods albeit at exorbitant prices.

The big risk to both, the crews and the freight on vessels sailing on this route, begins as they treaded along the Somali coast line up

Indian Ocean coast south of Mogadishu

to the destined shoreline or ad-hoc mooring or anchoring facility. Although protecting ships from local pirates or safety was the top priority, shoal areas and coastal reefs, which could vary in breadth depending on marine weather conditions, were the main hazards of maritime sailing in this part of the Indian Ocean.

In our case, the final destination was a point north of Mogadishu, called "Ceel Macaan", pronounceable in English as "El Ma'an".

An even bigger risk was how to transport the goods through treacherous terrain, mostly protecting the cargo from aggressive freelance armed gangs until it reaches the stores in Mogadishu proper.

Yet, due to the relentless efforts of Dr. Osman, the young assistants and associates he recruited in Mogadishu, the first shipment arrived and landed after a slight delay at Mombasa harbor. It was unbelievable how the delicate and sensitive freight made the tortuous maritime voyage without a single loss or a damaged item. This encouraged the partners on both ends to dispatch bigger consignments via the same route with, fortunately, more success and smooth sailing.

Success of the shipments' arrival and their fast sales turn over notwithstanding, it could not generate enough funds to support Hassan's family to remain in Cairo. In addition, the security situation in Mogadishu, although relatively improved, remained precarious and volatile. No one within his rational senses would hedge his bets to rely on it for a sustained and peaceful continuation of a regular profit yielding business.

Hassan made a renewed appraisal of his family's prospects and decided to look again for a safe haven which may allow him to work and provide for his family.

Woman with traditional scarf

As this was not possible either in Egypt or in Somalia, he had to set his sights again toward the west. His contacts in Germany was dealt a debilitating blow by the absorption of German Cargo Services, which made forth nightly flights to Mogadishu prior to the outbreak of civil war when he continued to have significant hope laden business until 1990, back into the fold of bigger Lufthansa Cargo in a major restructuring move by the top management.

This, coupled with the continually worsening situation back in Somalia, in effect, dashed any hopes for the kind of the solution Hassan was looking forward to.

The only option that remained was to get in touch with his friends in the U.S. While conducting his travel and trading agency business in Mogadishu during the '80s, Hassan also acted as a consultant for the Boeing commercial airplane group of Renton, Washington, where he forged excellent personal friendships with the executives who frequently visited Mogadishu over nearly a decade.

As early as 1992, Hassan wrote from Cairo to Boeing advising them of the inevitable expiry of his consultancy due to the closure of his business as a result of the civil war in Somalia.

He also got in touch with Mark Muhsam and asked him to convey his regards to his colleague David Axe, and to provide him with his current address if and when possible.

Although the address was received with the return mail then, it was not followed up by Hassan as he hoped matters will be improved back home with the arrival of international forces, at the onset of Operation Restore Hope.

Now after the Somali crisis has become hopeless and disaster prone, Hassan thought it appropriate to revive his contacts with his Boeing friends in the US.

He got in touch with Dave Axe first who wrote back, proposing that Hassan study the idea of representing a high tech new venture in Egypt that he now works for as a consultant and is owned or managed by a personal friend of his. Dave has retired from Boeing service during the latter half of the 1980's and has lived since in a rural like environment after moving to live in his own house at the small town of Index, an old mining center in the mountainous region of western Washington.

His children all grown up, he was mainly in SatScan Electronics Inc., to help out his friend Michael Lee and to make use of his time when he is not helping with his local new Methodist congregation which, sometimes, engages him in voluntary trips to villages, as far as Guatemala, where he helps install, sometimes single handedly, whole telephone projects through his creative electronics skill.

Being a good samaritan, he devised a perfect way to avoid the boredom that engulfs individuals in their retirement years and carved for himself a niche which enables him satisfy his moral and spiritual obligations and makes him busy at the same time.

Hassan took to this idea, which he envisaged could be the best way to make his stay in Egypt all the more worthwhile, even if it would only provide the basic financial needs for his family.

He embarked on conducting the research needed for introducing a pilot project to enhance electrical knowledge in Egyptian middle to high school grades and to encourage the educational system produce more technically prepared skills for the benefit of the Egyptian national industry. It was envisaged that the United Nations would encourage such endeavor in line with its policy of promoting economic development related educational projects in all developing countries around the world.

SatScan was also involved in developing high-tech satellite connected television weather forecast systems and had already made sales to some North African nations including Algeria.

When Hassan completed his research on the subject, SatScan invited him to visit their head office in Sultan, a small town in Snohomish County, Washington. In the meantime, Hassan continued his pharmaceutical import shipments to his associates in Mogadishu to keep the supplies flowing before departing to the United States to discuss his report on the existing potential for electrical / electronics sales to Egypt with the management of SatScan Electronics Inc., his possible future business associates.

Hassan arrived at Seattle International Airport by September 21st, 1997. Dave Axe was there to welcome his long time friend. Since his last visit to Mogadishu early 1985, the only contact they had was through mail. Dave went into retirement in 1988 and began devoting all his time to his family and his samaritan pursuits, still he found time to employ his talent in inventive contributions as a consultant to SatScan.

To Hassan's surprise, it was a warm sunny afternoon as the TWA flight approached the runway; the view of the surrounding environment was breathtaking. He did not expect to have a clear and sunny, warm weather. Instead he envisioned rainy, damp and wet climatic conditions overseen by snow capped and fir populated range of mountains.

The drive from Seatac, as the airport town came to be known after the construction and inauguration of the Seattle-Tacoma International Airport terminal, was breathtaking indeed. The lush, verdant environment seemed to be still glowing in a belated summer like buoyancy, although the imposing fir greenery was experiencing an early tinge of red and brownish autumn like incursions.

This was most vivid in that late afternoon, especially on the mountains facing the Pacific Ocean side where images of the sunset were engaged in playing a natural symphony of colorful harmony that can be seen by even the casual observer at this particular time and place. To be witness to this natural wonder, Hassan thought, was a blessing in itself.

As the faithful Subaru sedan flawlessly negotiated the scenic modern freeways and highways between Seatac and Index, Hassan was on the one hand, amicably exchanging the normal friendly dialogue which presents itself in similar situations, and on the other, he was completely overwhelmed by this mix of primordial natural beauty and modern technological advance.

He mused upon the fact that, whatever man tries to achieve in this universe, nature will be there to remind him of the power of the Creator. In addition to the magnificent natural setting, the exceptionally warm weather that particular afternoon also took Hassan by complete surprise.

By the time Hassan fully grasped the new reality they were driving through Sultan, where SatScan set its base in an old horse breeding farm with a small stream running nearby its small office, laboratory and storage shed.

As the car moved along highway 2, the roadside signboards and commercials were introducing Hassan to the new world he often read about or heard of.

The ostrich farm and reptile farm signboards were in display; there was also a salmon nursery. Then there was the ostrich meat restaurant. Hassan could easily digest an ostrich farm as something unique in an environment like the northwest of the U.S. One would probably assume it is there to supply zoos or the scientific and academic research communities, but to find ostrich meat served as game food really confounded him.

He remembered elders talking about how ostrich eggs were fanciful, decorative pieces for living rooms. He also saw ostriches freely and elegantly wandering in the savanna pastoral plains of his own native country. He never thought that one day he will come across a signboard inviting customers to a gourmet ostrich delicacy. Well, live and learn, Hassan silently pondered.

The car entered the final turn toward Index, a small two lane road leading to a narrow bridge over the seemingly shallow Skykomish River into the sleepy Index town. Engulfed by the Index mountain range from all directions, it gives the first time visitor the impression that somehow he is voluntarily surrendering himself to the inescapable might of natural forces.

The awesome heights immediately surrounding the tiny urban settlement and forming a menacing enclosure make one momentarily entertain a nightmarish vision of entrapment, particularly in the event nature unleashes one of its moments of rage in the form of, God forbid, an Earthquake, a calamity this area of the U.S. is familiar, with or even an enormous flood caused by a combination of melting snow and an abnormally tropical, "El Nino" like, downpour.

Once you get over the bridge, however, and move toward the more familiar scenery of the school, the general store and the local eatery, the first awesome impression gives way to the more realistic vision that you are in traditional small town America.

As the car turned the corner behind the general store and veered southward, Hassan glimpsed the two story house at the end of the street only three houses away. He was already familiar with the house. He followed the progress of its construction since Dave started it in the seventies when his frequent trips to the Middle East and East

Africa interrupted his efforts to complete it with a single handed effort, but could not diminish his determination to complete it well before his retirement.

A photo of the house with Dave and the youngest of his children Holly, then 11 years old, standing in the lawn was also kept in Hassan's family album. Having received it in an earlier exchange of personal correspondence, it was included not only as part of the friendly ties that gained strength with time, but also as a sign of support for the determined effort behind realizing the whole project. It stood, Hassan believed, as a monument for an individual's victory against all the odds, financial, bureaucratic and otherwise to build his retirement's nest, away from the big city's heartbreaking pace and other health hazards.

When the car finally parked by the backyard just short of the garage shed, Karen stood there, her face beaming with a sincere welcoming smile. As they disembarked, Dave began introducing Hassan to Karen and Shadow, the faithful poodle who keeps them company. Dave and Karen then led Hassan into the house and showed him his room.

Few minutes later Hassan joined Dave in the back yard porch for a cup of tea. Karen went quietly into the kitchen preparing for dinner. Only the day before Hassan's arrival, Dave drove Holly to her residence at the Seattle Pacific University's campus in Seattle where she just began her freshman year.

A lengthy transatlantic flight that began almost 24 hours earlier at Cairo, Egypt, notwithstanding, Hassan did not feel a bit tired. A hot cup of tea in a friendly and cordial setting were enough to invigorate his spirit and trigger an animated and sometimes nostalgic conversation, which brought up reminiscences of younger days when Dave and Hassan first met in Mogadishu and neither was yet attacked by baldness or slowed by the inevitable advancing age.

The Pacific Northwest was at the beginning of autumn but still within sun saving time enjoying the longer days of summer. The marathon conversation continued to be interrupted only by an exquisite, delicious dinner. Dave and Hassan then returned to the porch for more conversation.

Although Mount Index loomed majestically over the immediate horizon of the house, one could see the star studded skies in a clear cloudless night. Accustomed to scouring or surfing the Indian Ocean version of the Milky Way, Hassan was eager to have a searching look at the skies where the northern Polar Star and the Big Dipper took center stage and to take advantage of this rare opportunity made available to him by virtue of being with his friends Dave and his wife Karen.

After an enjoyable evening of animated conversation, delicious food and star gazing, it was time to retire. Everybody in the house, including Shadow, went to bed or so Hassan thought. In his bed, he thanked God again for the fact that wherever he set foot he found good people to take care of him.

He remembered, his mother's prayer was always centered on the sentence "may God make your life easier through good human beings". In retrospect he realized the wisdom of her prayers and, as it resonated in his memory, his belief in its power gained further strength. Minutes after, sleep took over. After approximately two hours, however, an ear piercing train siren broke up the eerie silence of the night, followed by a wolf-like howl and made Hassan jump from his bed to realize it is a passing train with an audible comment from Shadow, announcing her presence or whatever a fake canine wolf-like howl meant.

Later, Hassan learned this was a nightly ritual practiced by Shadow over the years. After this entertaining episode, which lasted for few minutes, sleep set in again and continued without interruption well into the next morning.

No appointments were scheduled until Monday. Michael Lee, chief executive officer of SatScan was expected to return from one of his frequent trips to British Columbia in Canada over the weekend. A meeting with him was scheduled.

Meanwhile, Dave planned several sightseeing trips around Snohomish and King Counties, including a thoughtfully inserted visit to one of the Somali ethnic restaurants were Hassan was able to relive a real Somali environment after nearly a decade.

The sightseeing itinerary also included several landmarks of the Puget Sound area, namely, Ballard Salmon locks, located at the point of convergence of lake Washington and Lake Union into the pacific where an elaborate system of locks was erected to enable this valuable natural resource continue its journey north, where it may eventually reach its spawning grounds in a yearly ritual unique to the species.

New Homeland

The Monday Mike Lee, Chief Executive Officer of SatScan Electronics Incorporated was expected to return from his retreat in Canada where his mother was born, did finally arrive. Dave and Hassan were present at the right moment. Mike met them in his usual work office-cum-laboratory outfit and began first explaining a various array of high-tech apparatus and other gadgets geared toward satellite meteorological services for ongoing weather forecasting projects in the North African area.

He then led both, Dave and Hassan toward other parts of the facility, showing them works on different projects being carried out by other technicians. There was also some talk about a lady who was in accounting but left the weekend before because her term ended.

After showing Hassan all the parts of the facility, they all settled in the privacy of the separate conference room, where Mike, in a business like manner, began expanding and exploring cooperation on several fronts, especially with the advent of the German project of assisting in upgrading the capabilities of Egyptian Technical Institutes, but he also emphasized the necessity of gaining the financial support and sponsoring of the United Nations for projects oriented to create Egyptian Technical Institutes, dishing out electricians who accept being trained with SatScan manufactured toolkit which may equip them for the kind of future work they intend to carry out in remote country areas of Egyptian hinterland.

This will also result in a mutually long term beneficial effect. Mike Lee insisted this was not the end game for the high-tech industry. It still remains a future oriented industry, ripe with abundant opportunities and exiting inventions, which might trigger the whole industry into a totally different shape and new direction but, by now, it has become a saturated and monotonously slow market. It will take a young, budding company a great deal of struggle to just survive. Hence, the requirement of a bedrock support from either an internationally recognized political organization or a famous financial establishment trusted by western institutions.

On the way back home, Hassan was slowly digesting Mike Lee's words. It was clear to him that SatScan does no longer have the ability or the stomach to invest and bank on uncertain future in a far away country. They thought at the time, it would be worth their while to invest more realistically in a closer political ground, i.e. the U.S.A. or Canada. From their perspective it may not be the right step, for an investor to let his investment and brainwork (intellectual property) perform overseas.

For his own decision making though, Hassan was thrown few steps back to ponder and to think about. He kept on digesting Mike Lee's words and started thinking of joining his Somali kinsfolk in down town Seattle the next few days.

He quitely advised Dave and Karen of his intentions. Dave was all the way eager to assist Hassan in whichever way he could. He has already gone a long way to make his stay in Washington State, his homestead, as comfortable as possible and was willing to do more. In fact, he was only awaiting from Hassan to express himself out and to eventually divulge his back up plan for his family's future.

It took Hassan few more days to make phone conversations with family and friends alike, until Mark Muhsam phoned directly back to Hassan, announcing that he was engrossed in one of his globetrotting sales campaigns for Boeing in the oil region of the Middle East. He shall soon arrive back and will, certainly, be in touch again.

And so it happened. Meanwhile, Hassan got in touch with his ethnic Somali friends who agreed to pick him up.

It was there and then, when Hassan finally decided to move down to Seattle, WA. Eventually, Yassin Kediye, Saed Duale and another young man leaving urgently for San Diego came to pick him up for a Somali style bash, coinciding with the recently fresh marriage of Yassin and Isir.

Shortly afterward, Mark arrived back in Seattle and made the promised phone call to Hassan at his recently established Bachelor's pad with Mohamed Jama and Khalif.

The phone call was incredibly genuine. Mark made no bones about the transfer. He made it immediately clear, he is ready to host Hassan at home until his own family enters the U.S.A. at whatever pretext. He also indicated all his own kids, both Mathew and Heidi, his biological offsprings and his stepdaughter Vet. Dr. Lisa Scherr, his second wife Katie's own daughter, have all finished schooling and live their own lives around Seattle.

Hassan listened carefully and had only one remark to note on this tremendously generous offer. Hassan said, generally in Somali culture, only ladies are responsible for the home stay of any guest.

Mark was ready for any eventuality. He told Hassan, without any question he has his full unqualified trust, he was absolutely certain that Katie was more of a humane kind than he is. He shall discover no ill feelings, what so ever, during his stay in their midst.

Hassan also spoke to Katie over the same phone who welcomed him likewise even with a better and more encouraging enthusiasm. This made Hassan feel highly comfortable.

The next day, Katie came with her black Blazer and picked him with his travel baggage up to Bellevue. Finally, Hassan met Mark in person after he returned from one of those urgent sales meetings at Boeing. Mark, at first, was mainly concerned about Hassan's personal welfare; other things were to be looked at later, or in private.

Katie proved to be the perfect, humane sister to be found any where. She gave him the most adroit welcome to be given to a family guest waiting for his loved ones to eventually arrive and join him in the country. She also ensured he feels comfortable in his wing in the house without the slightest intrusion. She created the correct atmosphere for a person of his culture. Apparently her educated experience as a wife of a globetrotting salesman paid handsomely in the circumstances.

Hassan felt totally at ease and finally settled. Encounters, cordial, social and family visits of the various dispersed members of the kinsfolk came gradually and at a latter stage.

In one of the more interesting social events, Helena Muhsam joint them, the senior matriarch "Ummi" or "Granny", an old twisted Arabic term, probably introduced by Turks during earlier times, when they attacked Hungary or parts of western Europe, and attended a big family's introductory and welcome bash.

She proved to be an interesting matriarch. Originally from Ohio, where she first landed and grew up, she almost single-handedly educated her own and only son Mark, until he completed the Naval Academy as a navigator and finally settled in Seattle, working his way up at Boeing as an international salesman. Mark's relationship with his, also originally Transylvanian, Dad was slightly remote and perfunctory, or at least, that is what he understood in one of their conversations.

After some time, "Ummi" turned out a flurry of home-made or "Timiswaran" cooking. Later on normal visiting patterns amongst relatives, children and parents continued in a usual familiar manner.

Occasional and timely visits sometimes came from the Crockers, Drs. Evan and Lisa Crocker and from Heidi and Randy Stoupher with their kids Sara and Brayden. Also from Mathew, sometimes with his friends. Often, he settled at home in the absence of Mark.

Those paid visits to the house, especially in Mathew, Lisa and her Husband's case, during Mark and Katie's frequent trips to the eastern hemisphere, to assist in household chore's were very helpful.

The temporary residential arrangement was ideal. Hassan never felt a stranger, never felt lonely at any time in that house.

Incidentally, by now and actually for some time, Lisa was married to Dr. Evan Crocker, who is originally from somewhere between Northern California and South Oregon.

Not in any way shedding their own hosting responsibility toward Hassan, both Karen and Dave continued to pay their very frequent visits downtown, Bellevue, for either health or status follow-up. They both did an excellent job there; replenishing any shortages he faced whichever way it mattered. As Hassan himself repeatedly confirmed, the hosting preparation and arrangement was simply ideal.

Hassan, in the meantime, continued to talk on the phone with Khadija and the kids in Cairo almost weekly. It took him almost two years waiting for his family to arrive.

Throughout this whole period and, in spite of the frequent trips which both Mark and Katie undertook in their, sometimes, hectic involvement with international travel, he never felt lonely. As soon as the house was vacated, one or two other members of the same family either filled in, or visited the big family home daily to keep company to Hassan or to help in normal house functions. Other social accomplishments were naturally included.

Meanwhile, in Cairo, matters were not clearly magnified to the local American Embassy until the UNCHR resident of Egypt's Office passed on details of the current Somali stranded families in Egypt to be transferred to the rare and the few world communities who were kind enough to accept incoming civil war / displaced and stranded foreign families in their midst..

Miss Caroline, the officer in charge at Cairo's U.S. Embassy investigated Hassan's family case, along with a visiting Immigration and Naturalization Service (INS) delegate.

After ascertaining the existing facts, they decided to allow them be transported, in cohesion with international humanitarian organizations sponsored by the UNO, and accept Hassan's family among the genuinely stranded Somali families, for a long time, in the fold of advanced and settled communities as previously arranged with the UNO.

The family eventually landed in Seattle, where Karen, Dave and Hassan were awaiting with flowers and grant them the warmest welcome of their arrival to the North West.

Prior to their arrival, Dave worked very hard with Hassan and the International Rescue Committee (IRC) to find a suitable apartment, locating one in the end.

Dave also assisted Hassan considerably to find a convenient family transportation. A used family sedan was found and bought both for work and family needs.

Ali Hufane, the case worker at IRC originally a Somali, now a U.S. citizen also assisted considerably in agreeing with the landlord after the arriving refugee family settled to their final destination.

Karen, Dave and the visiting daughter, Kirsten, with her young grandchildren Paul and Benjamin, gave them a delightful luncheon in their quarters at Index.

Hassan then returned the family to their new address. Katie and Mark came in and provided all the needed utensils at home and some of the household and essential furnishings. Mark also helped Hassan purchase in a garage sale a used living room. In this manner the new arrival's life in Seattle began.

Given the fact that, Somalia having truly become in the latest category of modern political history, the first western inspired nation failed state, in most aspects, in one of its episodes of total disintegration, there was a general opinion within the Headquarters of the U.S. Foreign Department that Somalia now resembles and almost reverted to what the Wild West looked like during the 19th Century.

Hassan's family had a lot to contend with being newcomers to an entirely different culture. Hassan discovered, whilst going through the legal corridors of establishing a newcomer's foothold within the

U.S. as a normal refugee or citizen, life is not as easy to sail through as it is in his own culture. It is also much more difficult to get introduced or easily absorb a new culture's life long learned ways of living, particularly at a later stage.

After their settlement and initial introduction into life, as usual, children went their ways. Minors were immediately inducted into normal elementary, middle or "English as a Second Language" (ESL) schooling.

Adults dispersed into various mostly menial jobs. Life in a different culture means many things, as reality turned out. Unless you have already been academically qualified in economically competent profession earlier in the past, you are going to suffer the downsizing indications of doom.

This is almost what happened in this instance. There are also hard facts one faces even at lowest levels. It is an authentically different culture.

When Hassan tried to approach his old partners at Boeing Company in Seattle, Wa. through his local friends during 1998, Boeing, at that time still seated in Renton, Washington, had already completely acquired its Long Beach based behemoth, McDonnel Douglas, and added its complement to its own work force.

Then, suddenly, with a down turn in the subsequent international aerospace market due to various reasons, began reducing an enormous number of employees and implementing high-level restructuring. It also discouraged any newcomer, especially with a very traditional relationship like Hassan's, for new positions. Simply there were none.

After the expiry of the initially Social Security Bureau introductory period, and after attending an entry level course at one of the local community colleges in Washington State, again with a massive help from the Axes, Hassan simply sought one of the menial jobs available planning to survive in preparation, prior to the arrival of the family.

Schoolgirl with scarf in Bossaso

History

Somalia's Political History

It is more easier to say than to prove in terms of a realistic and genuinely current historic context that the recent and present Somali national debacle represents a turbulent, heavy weight factor in the international political events, either worldwide or at least in the regional area of the Middle East or the strategically vital region to Europe and to the U.S. of overseeing the waterways to the Gulf oil producing area of the Indian Ocean as a whole.

Any serious scholar has to go back in history and deeply delve into the annals of ancient historical background prior to just attacking Somali rulers of recent, past or current periods of that country. When this is worked out, only then, one may arrive at a certain conclusion.

The largest obstacle in tracing Somali political history and culture was, remains, and shall always be the total lack of Somali orthography in past decades. This fact, alone, did place Somalis in a unique situation. Scholars and students of history alike wonder, most of the time, whether they could pinpoint a particular era, epoch or period to state at which the Somali fold independently moved out of the geographically, ethnically and linguistically dominant Hamitic race, spanning the whole eastern region to the northern edge of East Africa and to the Berber region in the Atlas mountains of Morocco, including Ancient Egypt's valley of Wadi Halfa, which is geographically positioned, mostly, in northern Sudan with the internationally famous Ancient Egyptian temples of Abu Simbel, half buried within the northern most tip of today's Wadi Halfa, but now recognized as Upper Egypt.

The indigenous language amongst the original Nubian citizens of Abu Symbol, Kom Ambo and Bani Mazar in the Aswani Upper Egypt region remains the original Cushitic, or Ancient Egyptian language. It is the Nubi original (language and culture), not English translation of today.

It is also spoken, to a certain extent, by the nomadic Bashayira and Ababida, mainly camel herding tribes, who cover the area spanning Upper Egypt and the north eastern territory of Sudan, where the Sudanese Beija Nubian group have been herding and living since times immemorial.

It is one of the main reasons why the Sudanese-Egyptian authorities are still engaged in a conflict over a territorial southern Egypt and Northern Sudan dispute, which lingers on since two centuries when the British colonized and ruled that part of Africa.

Another time bomb.

Not to sink further into the origins of the Cushitic Group of Ancient Egyptians. We must move forward in history when Somalis finally emerged in modern times as a separate local Abyssinian race, integrally more mixed with south western Yemenites or the Himyarite pre-Arab Bedouin Culture blend of the human race of Ham-Sam who straddled both sides of the present Gulf of Aden and intermingled in a historically undocumented era.

In the more recent age of the 16th Century the Somali people first appeared through privately held manuscripts by European Renaissance collectors. The Somali Embassy in Cairo, Egypt, published officially to the general public during 1974 a book recording the eventful but eventually failed attempt at defeating Christian Coptic monarchies in Abyssinian highlands, and at the same time widening Islamic power in the eastern and southern Abyssinia.

It was highly suspected by the Somalis, at the time, that the ruling junta had a particular message to convey. The emergence of the Somalis as a distinct race, sudden as it was, amongst other Abyssinians, rather started much earlier through an ambiguous burst of tribal proliferation along the north eastern Escarpment of the East African Rift Valley. They spread down the East African savanna countryside, pushing their own Cushitic brothers, the Oromos, from their habitats at the presently Galka'ayo and Caabud Waaq towns, until they were finally halted by British colonizers with their traveling camels before reaching the limit they set for their own British segregated settlers.

After their sub-clans settled as a fully fledged Somali race, the originally Arabian Islamic warrior Ahmed Ibrahim (Alghazi), meaning in Classic Arabic "The Conqueror", first descended on Sa'daddin Island in Zeila on almost the north western border of today's Somalia during the realm of Awdal Sultanate of Sa'daddin family. He was recently glorified as a great religious warrior by the Siad Barre regime but actually failed as a conqueror. He may also have won the admiration of the then Tigrean-Amharic monarchies. He was famously known as "Ahmed Garan " in Ethiopia and as "Ahmed Gurey" in Somalia.

Inaccurate as they stood in the 16th Century, many details about his battles and life are bound to cause a great confusion today.

It was suspected, he may, haphazardly, have been mentioned in the officially published book by the late Somali junta of Siad Barre in 1974, as another Somali leading warrior against the Christian monarchy called "Ahmed Gurey" Hussein of the Habar Mugdi or Berrei Somali sub-clans, who initially resisted the domination by the Ottoman conquest but finally lined up with his kinsfolk to liberate the Christian part in favor of the Islamic conquest on mainly western Abyssinia.

It could have meant also that a Marehan sub-clan leader namely Harabou Gweta Tedrous Adam, did assume the Somali leadership even in the ancient past.

Since Siad Barre himself belonged to the Marehan sub-clan, this sentence refers to the message his regime wanted to convey to the Somali people in the book that an earlier member of his sub-clan, historically, did assume a position of leadership.

It is a matter of conjecture. It was rumored then, the main reason for asking the Embassy in Cairo in the 1970's to publish this book was to demonstrate Marehan's leadership ability. One of the significant advantages for including this name was tied to that rumor. It is not certain that a neutral reader would buy that argument.

Another historical significance that one derived from reading this book was that the name itself did reflect an obvious Abyssinian connection and ancestry in those days.

The proper Ahmed Garan either might have migrated or descended through the heavily Ottoman filtered Awdal Region of Zeila. However, he subsequently won the power struggle in Somalia itself, by subjugating the "Sa'daddin dynasty in Berbera on religious reform terms", prior to launching his Islamic rebellion against the Christian monarchies reign over Abyssinia.

Somali tribes, especially the Geri Amlaleh of the Darod clan, who became his immediate in-laws, were lined up behind him, and so were all other Somali sub-clans who saw an overall and grand salvation in his plan. They were already Moslems in belief, as they emerged earlier in a rather hazy dark age but, having an overwhelmingly Bedouin way of life, environmentally and socio-economically did not fully conform to the modern technical outlook or civil way of life. They found it profoundly difficult to adapt to western ways of living and technical advancement.

Ahmed Garan's conquest to convert the Christian Abyssinians to Islam was just one of the last religious battles. Although it was observed that Italy's religious records indicate they successfully scored for their Christian allies in Africa, which may have amply served Western Powers later throughout the 20th Century Cold War battle with the Soviets, it is more likely that the Portuguese did in fact materially assist the monarchy's war effort to thwart all the attempted conquests. The burning of the Zeila port on the northern Somali coast in the year 1516 by Portugal could have been part of the same material support at the time.

In any case, the initial hunt and the colonizing of rich Sub Saharan Africa by European powers began rather slowly in the 16th Century. Its fallout and reverberations are still being felt today. Somalia, in the immediate colonial sequence, which it was subjected to by fate, despite some internal resistance from local rebels, ended up as a terribly mutilated colonial property.

The British Victorian Empire's decline and its ever changing colonial strategies back in Westminster did eventually affect their destiny on several occasions, including the Ernest Bevin (then Foreign Minister of the Labor Government) offer to the "League of Nations" in 1949, to reunite the Somali Protectorate in all its five parts, provided they joined the British Commonwealth.

Both the French and the Soviet governments flatly rejected it as an exercise in imperial expansion. Even the WWII statesman Winston Churchill was inconspicuous during his stint as a Minister of Colonies.

Somalia emerged as separate, in a typically Dark Age when all demographic, environmental and socio-economic upheavals occur, and may cause highly notable changes in any society. In the Somali case, its immensely proud Bedouin culture simply fell victim to its own ignorance. Torn between several different European imported western systems, which essentially were alien to its own Bedouin camel influenced original culture as a vital ingredient of Somali life.

Its rule suddenly fell into disrepute and was already an irreparably damaged vehicle by the time they rebelled against their last despot.

Somalis shall not recover from the mess they are involved in now, unless they agree on burying the hatchet and become united on a clearly honest path they chart for themselves in the immediate future.

Western Colonialism's Real Damage
to the Independent Somali State

Somalia was already victimized and divided as colonial convenience dictated. Eventually, Somalis were united within the tutelage of the United Nations Trusteeship supervision during the 1960's for what is known until today as "Somalia proper". Initially, their predicament began with the establishment of a European or western style democracy that failed at birth.

What exactly happened was that the public at large did not comprehend the essence of the cultural mentality which was basically modeled on a modern system of a civilian civic sense and a Hellenic-Roman heritage.

Somalis live in an entirely different culture neatly tied to a Bedouin base of their own hinterland. They need an honest management of their resources. They also nurture a disdain for all industrial and hard working effort. They love contemplation, a Bohemian way of toying with nature and a sensuality which had been abandoned ages past.

The harsh, purely material world determined by a global race, instantly revolutionized by information technology, plastic money deals and stock exchange markets are still beyond their concepts.

Therefore, all Somali or similar neighboring rulers only took hold of a strong grip on the shell of power they usurped or inherited, and not only understood from the outset but mastered ways to hold on to it, so that a particular semblance of authority, indicating an internationally and diplomatically acceptable mode by the current world community at large, is conformingly and regularly displayed on the international arena.

Somalis are now standing nowhere. Only an empty shell, as a result of their confusion between two far in-between cultures. An ever technologically advancing culture of gigantic leaps, which is still continuing its march toward scientific discovery.

Arabs and their memorable Islamic might, who prior to the present civilization held immense sway over continents throughout the now medieval past, from the Far East into western Europe "Iberia" with its relative material and philosophical advances, but eventually degenerated into disarray until the final defeat of the Ottoman Empire of Turkey.

See in the "Qur'anic Revelation", Sura number 30, "The Romans". The first sentence shall tell you the whole version (1) (2) & (3) etc. Move on to its original complete content.

Immediately following the conclusive conferences of Potsdam and Yalta, and after the famous Suez Canal respite by President F. D. Roosevelt, the fate of the British Empire legacy was passed on, on a traditional baton, by the weary British post Victorian Empire to the new Western World superpower or New Deal U.S.A.

It was to be introduced to the new world order with particular provisos, protecting its secrets, interests and leadership of the nascent world and to be applied to everything else which mattered and/or happened throughout the subsequent events, unfolding later on an international scale including the subsequent long drawn exercise, which divided the world for more than half a century, when it finally forced, on occasions, NATO and Warsaw Pact armed forces to stand against each other in an act of global brinkmanship.

Somalia finally fell as the first despotically unsettled local African state, mainly for its private internal reasons of conflicting, despicable local economic failures or regionally created destabilizing factors utilizing both local governance failures and, partly, international and regional politics or even ethnic or cultural competency factors on certain occasions.

Somalia was different from other 1960's nascent states only in one internationally exposed aspect. It was the first Guinea Pig to fall victim as the now proverbial "First Failed Modern Western Style State".

Whether this is an asset or a failure of modern prevalent culture remains to be judged wisely. It also remains for all modern political scientists and theorists to research and to closely put its experience under the microscope for historical and/or future study.

A Brief View on Clan History*

The Darod: Oral History

The Somalis were, probably, first called by the following name, as a result of their almost complete dependence on the camel as a domestic animal for their subsistence and way of a Bedouin nomadic life. As the story goes, it originated with the word "Soo maal" or in English "Go and milk the she camel". They all lived together on the north eastern escarpment of the Horn of Africa.

Moving nomad family

As oral literature says, Darod or one of the major Somali patriarchs, is in reality AbdulRahman, the son of Sheikh Ismail Alghabarti, whose grave was conjured up earlier somehow on a tiny Islet just outside the tip of Berbera port across the Gulf of Aden.

But as a matter of fact he was buried at the south western Yemen coastal town of Zabid. His ancestral roots are linked to Aqiil Bin Abi Talib of the Quraishi Arabic tribe and a first cousin of Profit Mohamed. No reliable historical evidence was found. It may be based on a myth.

---

* See also Addendum: Genealogy of the Clans

Mr. Darod got married to a Dir lady in the name of "Dlonbero", as I saw the similarity in names of other ladies recorded in other books, living subsequently in the 16th Century, or "Donbiro" as Somalis pronounce it nowadays. She bore him several capable offspring who proliferated to become large sub-clans.

They played a major role in their earliest land grabbing and common pastoral territory widening forays on an all southward expansion, until they ended up at the forefront in all directions and, with some of their kinsfolk, in the Harar plateau region, down to the limits of "Isiolo" in the Northern Frontier District (N.F.D.), where Ogadeni and Bartire tribes are living alongside their Somali kinsfolk and other Kenyan tribes to our day.

The oral history of the Darod also has some sporadic written manuscripts, kept by private owners. It seemed, one of the main purposes of Siad Barre's leadership was showing the world, that a Marehan sub-clan leader did hold a Somali command during Ahmed Garan's attempt at conquering the whole of Abyssinia. The regime's intentions may have backfired politically since the Military Junta's policies were not popular. Historically, although Ahmed Gurey or Garan himself is still viewed by most Somalis as a heroic figure, his attempts eventually ended in failure.

The Hawiye: Oral History

Naturally, the Darod were not alone in settling at the Makher north eastern escarpment. In retrospect it seems that most of the Somali patriarchs were buried there. They were apparently cousins of the same racially mixed Abyssinians.

The Hawiye also dispersed down the savannah stretch to the southern limits of the riverine or "Webi Shabelle" area where other Abyssinian tribes resided in those times.

They also lined up for Islamic liberation of the western Christian monarchies behind Ahmed Garan, with the Darod, the Dir and the Isaaq.

Some of them also permanently inhabit now in the south eastern savannah of the Ogaden, like the Karanle and the Suleiman of the Habar Gidir who recently settled in the Wardheer area as a result of the last regime's pressure on them.

The Hawiye oral history was buried somehow within Somali mythology, until it emerged very late in the 20th Century during their last political uprising against the Siad Barre oppressive regime. They also revised more of the Hawiye central area tribes' history, who might have been commonly dispersed, but were mostly Italian colonized tribes of southern Somalia including parts of the "Sheikhal", hitherto regarded by all Somalis as a run of the mill, ethnically neutral, religious middle-men.

Their clan genealogy also shot up to Aqiil Bin Abu Talib as an ancestor.

No evidence of that, another probable myth.

The Isaaq: Oral History

Just like their other relatives, the Isaaq clan moved to the northwest and toward the Hawd area in the southwest, mingling with their mostly Darod cousins.

City of Berbera

They also settled in large urban areas like Hargeisa, then known as "Quarni", and may be Harar or in Sheikh, a small town on the northern escarpment south of Berbera, which at the beginning of British occupation served as their summertime alternative Capital to Berbera port, and during the 1930s became nationally known as the site of the only secondary school in the northern regions, including Bur'ao and Erigavo.

They increased their territorial expansion, both demographically and politically in all of the above towns and surrounding regions totally or partially.

Amongst the Somalis, the Isaaq prefer to be called as descendants of Sheikh "Isxaaq", pronounceable in English as Sheik "Is'hak", as it suits their

Man from Sheikh

recent Asian identity. Non Isaaq Somalis overwhelmingly use the "Isaaq" name for its linguistic commonality.

It is rumored amongst other tribes that they devised their own vision of lineage early in the 1940's, linking their ancestry to an Arab from Hadramout in South Yemen called Al Sheikh Is'hak Bin Ahmed, also, shooting up to Aqiil Bin Abu Talib.

Possibly another myth as there is no evidence of that either.

Since the SNM front declared secession of the northern regions following the ouster of the Siad Barre regime from the rest of the country, they have been attempting to demonstrate their territory as more stable and democratically governable than the Somali Salvation Democratic Front (SSDF), United Somali Congress (USC) and Rahanwein Revolutionary Army (RRA) controlled territories in the formerly Italian colonized part of southern Somalia.

The Dir: Oral History

Being probably the first Somali clan to decline attributing its ancestry to South Arabia, in Somali history Dir is reported to be the father in law of Darod. Likewise the Issa's who still form the Djibouti Republic's ruling class today, straddling the border toward the eastern town of Zeila into Somalia and the Samarons who live along the north western highlands, are also part of the present day racially undiluted sub-clans.

Coastal town of Mait

They never admitted in their oral history of being other than Somali Abyssinians. They remained residents of their true habitat.

Both Issa and Samaron ancestors were also buried in Mait alongside their relatives on the Makher or north-eastern coast of Somalia. Well before the Awdal Sultanate's Sa'daddin family reign, they lived in the Zeila coast all the way along the old caravan route of the 19th Century through Diri Dawa to Harar, in the eastern region of the present Ethiopian People Democratic Revolutionary Front (EPDRF) controlled country.

During the early sixties, however, some Somali politicians devised the Irir ancestral formula. It was related then that in Somali oral tradition it is supposed to represent a group of clans other than the Darod, whose patriarch was the first to claim that he came from Arabia. They included the Isaaq, Hawiye, Dir, Issa, Samaron, Biyamaal and the Dir.

One is not sure, whether this was a genuine political stroke, or whether it was a way to counter the Darod's quasi perpetual monopoly of being Somalia's top leaders.

During the seventies of the 20th Century, the Djibouti Republic became an independent country. It has an agreement with France which manages the southern Red Sea strategic base.

Somalia proper remains disintegrated, Djibouti's recent peaceful mediation efforts notwithstanding.

Port of Mait

Somali Lower Cast Clans

Somalis are tribally divided into different casts, known as "Sab", meaning 'lower cast', and "Aji" or 'mainstream' cast wise. The Sab who are considered a minority amongst Somalis, may have belonged to a collection of ancient or even pre-Somali tribes that were defeated or decimated in the deep dark history of the nation, and subjected afterwards according to ancient tradition or custom to carry out all the duties regarded as menial by the Somali Bedouin culture. They include the Midgaan tribe who attribute their ancestry to a patriarch named Musa Deriyeh and were traditional hunters, but are now mostly engaged in leather work (shoe makers) etc., the Tumaal tribe who traditionally functioned as blacksmiths, and the Yibir tribe who traditionally performed as sorcerers.

Incense-tree on Erigavo-Mait road

The only reference made to them was in a colonial British Somaliland Protectorate survey which was carried out late in the 1940's. They are all distributed among other Somalis in every region. They do not reside in a separate enclave of land. In urban areas, especially in Awdal until Sanaag or in ex British Somaliland Protectorate, they live in separate quarters. In the north-east down to Lower Juba or in ex Italian Somalia, they do not live residentially different from other Somalis.

They are also socially segregated against. They are not permitted by tradition to marry a daughter of the "Aji", which is against Islamic religion and all civilized codes.

They are not invited as equals to Somali mainstream gatherings. However, this was not strictly applied in the very recent past and has been disappearing since independence, as successive Somali governments made all types of segregation and discrimination unlawful and as education and modernity spread in Somali townships.

The following historical fact was found in the official manuscript, published by the then embedded Yemeni eyewitness to the battles of Ahmed Garan in Abyssinia during the 16th Century, Mr. Shahabaddin Aljizani. It records that "Yibir", a Somali clan, lined up behind the "Imam in South Eastern Bali" just like their other Somali kinsfolk.

It also clearly magnifies that circumstantial changes of the times may not necessarily obliterate the nature of peoples. It may, however, influence their lives to a great extent. The "Madhibaan" or lower casts, who together constitute some of the most industrious Somali or Abyssinian clans in the fold and who, under the degradations they endured amongst other clans in their society, can claim back whatever rights they feel deprived of. Only a time of healing and repentance will compensate them too.

Children in Scusiuban

Somalia's Rulers and Power Seekers

The Darod Rulers

While we remain focused on Somalia, we must continue to fall back on the fact that the Bedouin desert culture, especially accompanying the dromedary camel, had taken full hold of Somali life. Demographic and other developmental changes occurred as well.

In their earlier formation, apparently the Darod, having probably been the eldest of the new tribal breed, were the source of some legendary leaders and provided the traditional rulers. Whether this happened through a matter of fact or otherwise, in Somalia's traditional heritage they are considered the first breed of "Bedouin camel herder rulers".

During the latter periods of their rule, however, including the famous Mahdi-like uprising at the beginning of the 20th Century, which was basically an anti-colonialist religious campaign, that included all the Somalis at the start and continued until 1920 but ended in disarray and defeat, it seems in hindsight that the Somali people lost patience with a one man autocratic authority.

A begrudging feeling amongst other Somali tribes remained, as the Mijertein sub-clan in the north-east led the movement of the Somali Youth League (SYL) party toward national independence and unity in the 1960's, eventually occupying significant cabinet posts plus the presidency of the nation and dominating the Somali civilian governments for almost the first decade after the independence.

They were accused then by other clans of manipulating general elections to gain more seats in the National Assembly, and that they may have intentionally ignored to recognize the subsequent demographic changes, resulting in numerical dominance of their opposition in several regions, which divided the population and eventually weakened the civilian western style modern governments.

In the central area the Italian colonist Tomaselli's invisible line, drawn during his tenure in colonial days, may have afterwards lost its realistic touch on the ground because of demographic shifts in pastoral migration.

In addition, a requirement of regime change was felt by the masses, after Siad Barre stayed in power longer than anticipated, or as consequences of the dictatorial nature of his regime finally led to the break-out of hostilities and to the present state of disintegration.

Ina Abdulleh Hassan or "Sayedka" who initially rallied on behalf of the Somali people and included all tribes speaking the mainstream Somali language in his movement, was not only a "Mahdi of the Sudan" like or Ahmed Gurey like Islamic revolutionary, which prompted the English colonialists to call him the "Mad Mullah" at the time.

Raven over famous Taleh stronghold

He actually revolted against Somali children being forcibly adopted by the Christian clergy. Some of them were baptized in their infancy at Berbera and were shifted hurriedly afterward to the French colony of Djibouti. All Somali Tribes who are traditionally Muslims whole-heartedly supported him then.

Not only that. At first, he made a great headway from his hinterland forte with his Yemeni and Pakistani labor and German technicians at Taleh.

Later on he attempted to dominate all Somalis on political and clerical (theological) grounds as well. Both of which failed.

The onslaught of colonial air raids into the Ogaden semi desert skies finally brought about his defeat. He subsequently died of natural causes.

Somalis, as it was realistically experienced later on, were still living in a tribally biased Bedouin culture, but were actually running a modern citizen and tax based civilian western style state which had some of its own prerequisites missing.

Ruins of Taleh

It did not work in the end. The Military coup d'état conducted by Major General Siad Barre's junta, late in the 1960's, in itself turned out to be an act of sub-clan preservation (Marehan in this case), when the cold war era politics rode the wagon of independence in the Third World. It only aggravated other clans' envy and hatred of the Darod.

Whether it occurred haphazardly or by design, Siad Barre's Military Regime extensively abused political authority and remained for more than its own natural and humanly acceptable term in power, until its collapse by the last week of January 1991.

The Hawiye Rulers

They had a provisional Aministrazione Fiudiciaria Italo Somalia (AFIS) Prime Minister in Abdullahi Issa, but his authority was heavily influenced by the Italians who were managing the UN Trusteeship prior to Somali unity and independence of July 1960.

This provisional administration was condemned by the Somalis at the time. They dubbed it locally as the "G.S.", alluding to "Governo Saad", the sub-clan of Mr. Issa himself, instead of its official Governo Somalo or Somali Government. The blame could not be attributed to locals only at the time.

Somalia finally gained independence, and Aden Abdulle Osman became the symbol of the state as President on July 1960, Italian style, similar to Italy's post WWII republic, but he left the seat democratically and peacefully, when his replacement took over the seat in 1967.

Woman with camel herd

General Aideed's campaign as a Somali Power seeker

As for Aideed, his own strategy was immensely and directly focused on local Somali politics. He was not at ease in all circumstances with any outwardly distraction. He just wanted to establish an exclusively Habar Gidir regime in Mudug and the central regions of Somalia first, eventually descend on the central and southern regions, where the Hawiye, Rahanwein, meaning "large group" in Somali mainstream language and the non-Darod "Maxaad Tiri" speaking people reside and basically sympathize with his overall aim of eradicating the hitherto domineering Darod clan.

He wanted to uproot the Darod legacy, whom he firmly believed that once earlier in the century during the colonial upheavals throughout WW II, they cleverly used their slight political advantage in the north eastern ports and imposed the same to overrun their southern brothers, only to spread further southward down to Kismayo and rule over the rest of the land.

All subsequent events to him were mere local politics. When the U.S. President Bush, just fresh out of the Middle Eastern war, came to the rescue on humanitarian basis, American local presidential elections intervened again. Presidential fate was to determine the final outcome of a basically relief operation.

Ostensibly, a failing US ally which became mired in intractable local politics, needed a quick saving of the famished and down-stricken in poor Africa to balance the effect of disastrous calamities in a tremendously volatile region which remains to this day one of the difficult equations facing international politics.

What Aideed catastrophically overlooked in what would have been a shrewd political move, which may have molded the common interests of the influential bases of both Mogadishu and the northwestern region's business communities at a very critical phase, during which they formed an essential part of his own core USC organization, was the fact that, because of earlier drastic sub-clan divisiveness and haste or political rupture in the Diaspora, the USC organization disintegrated and, by the time they came down to the Capital, they were entirely mutilated with no unified final goal.

All the USC wings rallied to one common aim. To bring down the Military Junta whose real purpose might be to continue holding the Capital and international recognition hostages for a longer period. All sub-clans especially of the USC acted in one eventually effective uprising.

The highly popular political heavyweights of the time were separately recognized, both locally and internationally, in the form of eminent personalities as Dr. Ismail Jimaale, Haji Musa Boqor, Mohamed Abshir, Ali Mahdi, Hashi Weheliye and others.

No matter whatever independence he showed in the Diaspora, he eventually relented by allowing Dr. Ismail Jimaale to request a defiant Ali Wardhigley, head of the USC in Addis Ababa at the time, to mediate with Ethiopian authorities on his behalf.

Aideed subsequently concluded a cooperation agreement with Abdurrahman Ahmed Ali "Tur" of the SNM in Warabeye inside the still Ethiopian dominated region of Ogaden. Then relatively agreed to be allied with a sympathetic Ahmed Omer Jess, who turned out later to be just a side kick of Aideed himself.

Belonging to a renegade Somali Patriotic Movement (SPM), he was a Military colonel who originally rebelled against General Morgan's (his true name is Mohamed Said Hersi) wild manners when he reigned supreme during his Military governorship of Hargeisa. He subsequently alienated his Reer Isaaq sub-sub-clan from the larger Ogadeni Darod sub-clan as his followers.

Ostriches in Somali bush

Afterwards Jess might have served as an honest lackey of General Aideed when his small contingent was pushed back to Kismayo.

He was accused by the dislocated and indigenous Darod people that, whilst in power in Lower Juba, 100 Mijertein and other Darod civilians were massacred. This happened in a violent attempt to drive a wedge between the Ogaden, some sub-clans of which had their own separate agenda to dismantle the despotic Siad Barre regime, and the rest of the Darod. His attempt might have backfired and eventually contributed to his failure.

Over and above all, Aideed, without securing political power in his hand first, went on to split the country into several regions between the USC and the SNM in an illegal manner. The SNM wanted to secede anyway.

Aideed's major political error here was to entirely overlook the situation of the already regionally and culturally self conceited North-Westerners or SNM supporters, believing in the fact, it is the Hawiye's legitimate turn to receive the leadership banner at the Warabeye camp. The SNM secessionist front wanted their separate entity. They were dug in at their hideout without consulting any one else.

In his haste to topple the Siad Barre regime in Mogadishu and in spite of all of this, Aideed eventually found himself desperately involved in a chase and hunt campaign of a personal case of "deja vu".

A hurriedly overlapped, disorganized and terrorized UNOSOM organization, which may have experienced for its first time an attempt by a newly practicing lone superpower, experimenting its long powerful global reach on a new African upstart but, apparently, lost interest in the whole enterprise when it found neither an international nor a regional political credit out of it.

To return focusing on the Somali debacle, a seemingly intractable and intrinsically puzzling local arena. It has been already so for a long period in recent times. No foreign mediation shall find an amicable solution which will satisfy all sides. Every International or regional neighboring factor must possess some axe to grind or a certain vested interest to pursue. No one is immune or neutral there.

On this count alone, Somalis will have to finally put their own house in order, or to settle back to their own devices. If not, they will have to chew around or rethink of a lasting solution until they find one of their own.

Some heavy weight protagonists in the region like Egypt's President Mubarak declared once at his own National Assembly during the mid 1990's after witnessing another fake reconciliation of the Somali feuding clans, that Somalia was suffering at the time of an acutely deteriorated and bad leadership. Sarcastic as it was, that was the real fact on the ground.

Aideed, notwithstanding his vehement attempt to oust Siad Barre and to rest the whole country out of the tight grip of the old fledgling regime, himself became a prey of his own divisive and relentless pursuit of a one-man "Habar Gidir a.k.a. Reer Garas" rule. This was not to be so.

His other fatal and major error from the start was to ignore the existence of a parallel force, named the Abgaal within the Hawiye, who happened to be his own tribal next of kin and who, by natural habitat, dwelt closer to the Capital and built their militia war strength within and around its surroundings.

Secondly, he overlooked the business community centered in and around the Banadir Region. The largest trading force in the country, where most international and commercial institutions performed the country-wide influential import/export dealings. It also formed the secondary base of the alternative civilian administration, who could have somehow introduced their erstwhile timely reconciliation if all other attempts failed.

Having become devoid of this political asset or reserve, Aideed, eventually, frustrated all UNISOM and the superpower attempts to "Restore Hope" to the failed nation state and succumbed to his adorable combat interference within the Wadajir area, a southwest of Mogadishu enclave, where factions of his own Hawiye clan finally got him late one Thursday afternoon in 1994.

Ali Mahdi, who lost steam or enthusiasm after the disappearance of his archrival from the scene, got fed up with the continued uncontrolled and rampant thuggery of his own Abgaal sub-clan militia around his household. He quietly joined his second family in Cairo after making some showy conferences with Aideed's son and heir Hussein.

He eventually ceded the reign of international power to Abdi Qassim Salad in the Djibouti mediation process, but tribally gave in to other Abgaal co-leaders such as Hussein Bod or Muse Sudi Yelahow of Wadajir fame, who is nowadays regarded as the present banner carrying warlord of the Abgaal sub-clan and as the biggest rival of the Habar Gidir in the Capital.

The son of Aideed, a member of the United Somali Salvation

Kingfisher

and Reconstruction Council (SSRC) in Addis Ababa, in an outfit which includes some prominent warlords in Somalia, who are supposed to form the backbone of the latest administration emanating from the recently created Federal Parliament as result of the last reconciliation effort by the United Nations Organization in cooperation with regional bodies and neighboring states in Nairobi, Kenya.

International interest have gradually been diverted toward focusing on more currently urgent matters, such as global terrorism and on attempts to prevent weapons of mass destruction threats. Somalia, internationally, might be a dead case, waiting to be revived off the shelf later.

The north western Somali parts are still mesmerized with the final collapse of the Siad Barre corrupt and utterly despotic experience in their lives. They have never seen like him. Had it not been for the USC efforts at the southern part of the country, his regime may not have been deprived of its locally strong infrastructure in Mogadishu at least for another bout. That regime, especially after it has been completely abandoned by western powers, simply collapsed in front of local warlords and neighboring conniving states.

It was already dying from within. No one is shedding tears for it.

One fact remains in the Somali unwritten phase of Bedouin or Cushitic history. The Somalis are products of the same breed. Only a very ignorant and backward race whose concept of a fair and consultative traditional "XEER", the Somali word for "Home Grown Traditional Law", has to be developed equitably and be made to reconcile with the fairest cultural and religious jurisprudence. Modern practices should be implemented at all levels permanently.

Mohamed Ibrahim Egal, interim Prime Minister of Somaliland Protectorate's independence, Prime Minister of Unified Somalia until the assassination of the second republic's President Abdulrashid Ali Shermarke and the takeover of Siad Barre's Military Junta on Oct. 21st, 1969.

The presidency of Egal of the northwest's secessionist republic is considered by most Somalis as an opportunistic way of holding on to power.

Bee-eater

Egal visited Aden, a British colony, during 1959 when it transpired that the colonial authorities were looking for a Somali polititian, who was unfortunately imprisoned for one month after being accused by the same authorities of drunkenness but had, most likely, some political motive to hold him captive for a while.

Egal, the son of northwestern Somalia's wealthiest landlord and trader, was moving to leadership of the most popular political party, the Somali National League (SNL) in the Protectorate and its locally more popular weekly newspaper "Horn of Africa", which was neither well published nor edited, but the majority of the Somali urban residents bought it because of the national fervor and due to the fact that Arabic was considered the language of the sacred Qur'an.

At the water well

His personal friends and close political allies, both agreed he is pro-western. Even some of his political foes admitted he is the most prominent politically talented person who recently emerged amongst the ex Somaliland Protectorate Isaaq sub-clan tribesmen.

He had amongst his own popularly based National Party (SNL) succeeded to take the leadership of the ex-Protectorate in a western designed modern democracy adult franchise election.

He eventually led a local cabinet delegation to Lancaster House in London to win the Protectorate its independence and eventual union with the southern part of Somalia, few days later.

Egal basically mastered two elements in politics, in addition to his other traits:

1. he was extremely generous in distributing political gifts and cash even of his own property in general to others;

2. he was talented in both oratory and in political lobbying at the Somali level. In spite of the fact that most Somalis were stunned at his urban upbringing and linguistic eloquence.

Apart from the above, Egal was adept at getting rid of his own competitors through normal political connivance. He was a run of the mill politician. He also abhorred Military Regimes as he was one of their first victims.

A first class opportunist that a country like Somalia would offer, he managed to distribute one of the most realistic political manifestos during the waning days of Siad Barre's regime. As he took part in one of the first reconciliation conferences, offered by the neighboring Republic of Djibouti during President Guled's tenure, he then declared to some North-Westerners, at the time, after a short hop of discussing matters at the goings on at Bur'ao, the North-West's Conference site, that most of Northerners were not ripe for reuniting with their southern brothers as yet. Yet he went ahead with the Djibouti conference.

In the second conference that was held in Borama, he joined the candidates and won over the leadership of the SNM and the North West's secessionist presidency in mid 1993.

From there on he started to campaign for the secession nail and tooth until his death in a South African Hospital in Pretoria in mid 2002.

Succeeding in a democratic election albeit of a tribally localized system, he has shown a lot of transgressions throughout his tenure as a leader of the executive branch and demonstrated flashes of impatience during the latter years of the secessionist movement, in particular, in the North West.

Egal will not even qualify as a good ruler. He might qualify as a clever North Western politician. He was a politician who would not mind sleeping in the same bed with opposing political foes for the sake of a leadership post in the cabinet. Forget about a sense of mission and principles in the political arena.

Corruption was the mark of his regimes. He even believed it was the best way to guide the public to toe his own line of policies.

Yet, because of his own personal traits, he remains the best of a terrible bunch of despots. Left to his own devices, a man like Egal was a genuine representative of his Isaaq tribe.

His way of juggling clannish and national sentiments was always tailored to his remaining in a leading cabinet post.

His main failing, like any local dictator, was not to accept any

Somali cemetery

candidate for better or for worse in his electoral territory. His main asset was his utter dislike for Military Regimes, although for the sake of his own survival instinct he would get along even with their lot.

Reflections

Deeper Thoughts and Perceptions on Ancient Somali Identity

This is a really serious theme for all Somalis, who are still surviving today around the globe but possess a highly concerned idea with regard to the privately held perception of their own being.

The mere thought of their Somali existence and unity must be their main "raison d´etre" of identity and of an entirely tribal loyalty, based culturally and almost totally sided toward one single major Somali clan life they endured since their childhood.

Some might say otherwise.

This particular background belongs to a guy whose both mother and father hailed from ex British Somali Protectorate then. They got betrothed as circumstances dictated at the British colonized vital bunkering station named Aden, close to the south eastern strait of Bab El-Mandab or Berim Island of the Red Sea.

The author was born months later in Berbera to a temporarily recruited British marine salesman during World War II in the year of 1942. He happens to be one of those who firmly believe he is part and parcel, flesh and blood of Somalia's Berbera.

Berbera port and town

It may be politically correct for those whose majority dominates, on the current political equations, to deny him a seat or otherwise through fair elections on the grounds of an adult franchise; but it must be free for all citizens living legally at the site and/or whose birthright gives them that legal righteousness.

It is the land of God. People must accept that as a fact. Others were born there too, either earlier or later, but those whose indigenous tribes dwell in the Berbera area for probably few generations now, do not exclusively own the port for the northern Isaaq tribe. They can simply claim that out of sheer numerical dominance, they, presently, form the political majority.

No matter how long it takes, all Somalis, including those who are presently still in the strong grip of internecine tribal bias or jealousy shall get rid of it.

Time will tell, once hatred is done with.

Somalis have always been strong believers in their own Islamic faith. In their very unique Arabian Peninsula Bedouin style culture as well.

They always had a strange mixture of a hinterland and a modern urban Middle Eastern mentality. Proud and fierce warriors as they were characterized locally.

Their historical background remains often unrecorded for sheer lack of authentic data. They were even victimized, mutilated at will, later on by foreigners.

They also suffered on top of all of that the demeaning fact of being divided as a race into five parts, as the European colonizers elected to carve Africa at will according to their own interests.

Egyptian historians, in one of their vanity ridden strides, once described Somalis in an "Al Mussawar historical report" during the mid 1990's as only part of a very recently Arab "race of the edge". There are also "Central" Arabs they said.

There is, however, no significance whether you are an Arab or not, except in sheer identity. We are all humans.

It is the Great Curse that befell their ancient Hamitic race or the Pharaonic Egyptian Empires, who defied the will of the "Majestic God, our Creator", but only managed to create mundane pleasures and attempted to gain perpetual survival in this predetermined mortal world.

This Great Curse continues until our time. It has also been confirmed by many subsequent factual, historical and religious events. There is a deeply divine secret there.

It is not the specialty of this book to put the purely political and historical aspect of it to further research. However, for our own chronological sequence, we may cross over down the historical lane to another greater curse, introduced by a tribally biased belief through the Semites in a culturally Bedouin south west Asian peninsula, and probably during the Dark Ages mentioned prior to the monotheistic religions of Christianity, Torah, and Islam. This was to be described by subsequent descendents or Himyarites, pre Arab bedouins with relatively scant cave relics.

We firmly believe now in the fact, when humans became conscious and aware of their own surroundings and identity, resulting in the interaction among Abyssinians and peninsula Arabs, Qahtanites or Ba'ida south western Yemenis from Arabia Felix, including Jezan and parts of Najran, that Arabs began to look at their Hamitic cousins as human beings of different pigmentation and of a lower cast racially.

Somalis, the author hopes, are aware of that now. It is known in today's English as color stereotyping. It is also described sometimes as racial profiling as practiced by Caucasians in the modern world. It has been already mentioned in Islam, the monotheistic religion emerging at that time, when it warned all humans not to discriminate each other by color.

It also told them "You can only be closer to the Creator if you prove to be the most devout religiously". Moreover, by believing in the normal sequence of the monotheistic three new religions, "Torah" (Pentateuch), "Old and New Testament" (The Bible) and "The Qur'an", Abraham had already and categorically informed his offspring and posterity that "Islam" or "Total Submission to God" should be their religion as a whole.

This is confirmed in the Qur'an. It is believed by all Muslims that it was and shall for ever remain a genuine medium of worship to the Creator. Abraham declared his own Muslim-ship with this understanding and instructed his posterity to follow suit in advance.

Qur'anic school

Meanwhile, we leave it to other historians, anthropologists and geologists of epochs' demographics to sift through the several facets of universal or earthly transformation, religious- or otherwise, in the region. Great changes occurred in them, amongst them the colossal defeat and dispersal into final oblivion of the great ancient Egyptian Empire. At the same time or almost subsequent to the development of the interaction between humans of a different color or pigmentation in our history, since the age of enlightenment began in the now Arabic peninsula.

The "Musta'riba" who were the more cosmopolitan of the Arab ancestors of the Rabi'a, Modhar, Nizar and other Quraishi tribes or "the infidels among them", were the main culprits for introducing the tribally biased, now famous social classic system, where an individual owes his allegiance to one tribal ancestor instead of a government, where a citizen owes his loyalty to a state.

They were also the ones, in their active and energetic mass movement throughout those dark and medieval ages, who mingled northward with the northern Babylonians, Assyrians, Aramaic, Armenians and Phoenicians and eventually with the Mogul race northern Asians in the Far East, who may possibly constitute today's Austrians and Germans and all Caucasians.

All told, the biggest cultural curse of race is officially defined in today's prevalent English dictionary under race, as:

1. each of the major divisions of human kind, having distinct physical characteristics,

2. a tribe or a nation distinct as ethnic stock.

As history keeps proving to us, past and current examples were and are still being provided in reality by the Semites, who are acting on the same role and are holding the whole universe hostage to their private land or plot dispute, mixing it up with Biblical traditions and claiming intellectual property rights to religion "which is the property of all Humans" as their own politically shared turf.

Slavery may have been there all the time since the Creator condemned humanity in the shape of the Biblical Adam and Eve when the Creator relegated them and pardoned them temporarily to descend as mutual enemies from Heavens to Earth.

Try to work sufficiently hard and win back favor in both devotion to God and the world at large, eventually to be chosen, through God's will to move either to one of the selected Paradises or to Hell on the Day of Reckoning, but their perennially Bedouin based peninsula culture did introduce the real system of a different pigmentation of slavery Black& White to the Middle East.

"The Slavery Curse" continued and was introduced this time to the East Africans by the Peninsula Arabs.

Our world has never been the same again. Hence, read on the following (free translation) of the Sacred Qur'anic Revelation: "One of his miracles is in the creation of Heavens and Earth, and is in the difference in your speech and color. These are examples for those who know." (Quoted from Rome: Sura Nr. 30, Ayas: 21 to22.) It was only as a way for humans to distinguish one race from another. That's all. It was not meant to enslave each other.

In the following decades, the focus for historical and civil development turned to the Islamic conquests and dominance of all beliefs and creeds across the world, Somalis and other Abyssinians included.

In the ensuing greater human mass movement and upheaval, no reliable historical data was to be found anywhere, and with no written Somali language available, a remote ray of hope and enlightenment appeared signaling the emergence of a religious message in the name of Islam which dawned on the north eastern shores of the Horn of Africa.

How the Abyssinians came to be divided into separate monotheistic faiths is not clear. What is clearly apparent today in modern Europe is that The Oxford English Language dictionary describes the Somali people as follows:

"Somali or Somalis

1. are Hamitic Muslim people of Somalia in NE Africa,

2. is the Cushitic language of this people."

Some subsequent English language dictionaries describe the Somali people as a mixture of Arabian and African stock and the result of the last wave of Caucasian and African intermarriage in that part of Africa.

Nomad from southern Somalia

Arab historians and chroniclers might have mentioned in southern Arabia's local literature the arrival of Swahili (or Coastal in mainstream Arabic language), meaning in this particular historical perspective the coast of East Africa. Arab invaders or settlers to this region, where slavery was blatantly exercised and amply exported without legal hindrance throughout the whole area, spread down to

Mozambique. Possibly, the same pattern was also implemented until it reached the hearts of West African borders.

Somalis as a haggardly tribal people and immensely Bedouin in culture, apparently the grand children of ages of Himyarite and Arab interbreeding, finally settled in some unknown combination of circumstances at the Horn of Africa's eastern fringes of the Rift Valley.

A vague idea emerged among Somalis, spearheading a new unrecorded local revolt within the Somali speaking folk, who were moving with their desert prone Asian dromedary camel and Arabian thoroughbreds (horses), which might have originally sneaked through Bab el Mandab shoal straits ages ago during or prior to the "Abraha Historic Elephant Year", when he attempted to conquer Mecca and was defeated by divine power through a wave of stone throwing flying birds, which annihilated his force in the midst of Arabia's desert and when our Great Profit Mohammad was born.

That famous defeat of "Abraha" was later recorded in the sacred Qur'an Sura "The Elephant", No.105.

In another part of the sacred Qur'an the profit is informed that "Bedouins are in the extreme of disbelievers and hypocrites".

In the Twentieth Century's recent history the Italian Emissary to their East African Empire Prof. Cerulli, indicated in his book on the territory that Somalis are believers of the Islamic faith, but he suggested the urban Somalis in coastal areas are more truthful to the religion than their Bedouin brothers in the hinterland.

The latter, meaning the Bedouin, may kill a human being for a she-camel, not considering the fact that Islamic faith does not allow the same. The human self is so sacred that the plaintiff may settle for various mundane alternatives, such as monetary compensation or Diyah, which means a legal compensation either in cash or in kind "livestock especially in the case of nomads" for a human murder victim to his or her next of kin. It is spelled out in the Qur'an also as an alternative to capital punishment of death and putting an end to further bloodshed among tribes.

This may explain the fact that some Bedouin Somalis as their ancestors remain confused until today. It also magnifies the fact that local custom conflicts sometimes with religion in a significant manner.

At any rate, the influence of the camel culture is now worth considering in our present political impasse. From the strongest cultural and historical traces of recent Somali history, the camel and its Bedouin culture carries the total weight of a predominant Somali heritage.

As important now as it is, whilst fervently or calmly looking for a solution, one must always keep in mind that Somalis finally emerged on the modern times' political arena as very distinct Cushitic people, roaming for waterholes, rain water and pasture on the Horn of Africa's mostly plain and often highly rugged and slightly cool Rift Valley.

Somalis then spread in hordes toward all directions, probably just before the 13th Century, pushing other Cushitic speaking tribes, such as the Gallas who are today famously recognized as the "Oromos", and have been sponsoring a popular movement as a major component of the people who always existed in "Abyssinia proper" for more than thirty years. The current symbolic President of Ethiopia is an Oromo.

The Germans and the British after their colonial power grabbing initial surveys shunned it mostly. They chose the Kenyan and Nilotic Uganda and Tanganyika lands instead.

In an afterthought Lord Delamere of Imperial Britain launched a caravan trek by foot from Hargeisa southward to decide the depth of British Somaliland Protectorate.

Having been humiliated, mutilated and victimized and tribally Bedouin, ignorant and as proud as they were in their own blissful way, they happened to be oblivious to the devastating modern damage being inflicted by the relentless onslaught of the New Masters, the Europeans, in this era who modernized the chosen parts of the colonized African landscape in their own style, but in the process they also imposed their own culture, obliterating the African people's own historical heritage in a brutal way.

In this case they are not much different from other previous cultures. As Somalis suffered, separately, under the auspices of colonial powers they finally developed into a mutilated entity, divided into several parts artificially created by foreigners in Europe who chose to neglect it in the process, aiming at much richer and prosperous golden catches.

Still, Somalia's destiny remains in its peoples' own hands. Unless they agree on an amicable solution they shall remain in tatters for years to come.

Let us hope, a final solution shall arrive in the hands of a new generation, liberated from the present endemic hatred which inexplicably engulfed the present Somali elders.

Mother and son

Conclusion

The Somali debacle still continues after more than 14 years of Civil War, mayhem, warlord fiefdoms and total tribal chaos that has transformed the nation, once considered by others the most ethnically hegemonic state in Africa, into the "first nation failed state" at the heels of the collapse of the international Cold War which dominated the world political scene following World War II.

In spite of the fact that several international and regional conferences have been held to form a totally unified Somali government including the last interim administration recognized by the United Nations, Somalis are still divided and the nation is in total disarray.

All foreign efforts have so far failed to convince anyone of their true unifying good intentions. Some highly influential UN member governments are hoping, the latest interim Federal Administration shall provide the needed basic adult franchise requirements.

A presently negotiated final settlement sponsored by the Inter Government Authority on Development (IGAD), a regional organization under UN auspices in Eldoret, Mbagathi at Nairobi, Kenya, is already being opposed by some factions in Somalia. This was expected anyway.

The fact remains, however, that foreign powers formula, engineered and tailored to local needs, no matter how sympathetic and understanding from the outset it may look, shall never provide a lasting solution to the Somali local crisis.

At the onset of freedom early in the 1960's some "experienced colonialists", British colonial officers, who were responsible of Somaliland at the time or prior to it, and their supporters used to point out the fact that Somalis shall not be able to manage a western style democracy.

Only at a very late stage people realized, if those gentlemen were talking about the different alien culture the majority of the Somali population belonged to, which is essentially a Bedouin culture, then they were telling the truth.

During the nine years of civilian western style democratic rule, border skirmishes with neighboring states occurred, general elections were rigged by the central government in Mogadishu, local government status was neglected to be built realistically within the state apparatus and a national president was assassinated. In addition, opposing political figures were jailed when it was convenient.

The nascent elected National Assemblies and the executive governments failed to address the deeper cultural disparities between the western style suggested democracies, which most urban locals saw as ideal and contemporary for lack of comparative civil equivalents or as long as the international community welcomed it . But the reality was and still is that the majority of Somalis have a Bedouin culture very much closer to the Southern Arabian Peninsula one.

What was needed and may still be needed until today is a genuine reconciliation between that system and modernity. We all know that one of the biggest conflicts in the field of local policy making was the management of local governments or municipal councils.

The central governments in Mogadishu could not bring themselves up to get rid of their lust for local dominance by shedding local power to the local councils and by limiting local power to locally elected provincial or regional governors who represented both local and central rule.

The truth of the matter was that the majority of Somalis from the hinterland were utterly neglected and were left to their own devices to carry on living.

The central government remained in the belief, they could be conveniently manipulated during national border campaigns by igniting nationalistic sentiments to protect their waterholes and pasture from neighboring enemies or foreigners. They also counted on their tribal support when national elections were being held.

Apart from the fact that no tangible effort was made to help them out of their miserable lifestyle, elected officers and bureaucrats in the Capital thought they lived in Paradise. They turned the National Assembly and the colonially established civil service into a fixture of national industry which siphons national income including internationally received economic aid, enriching elected members each according to his political clout in the prevalent administration.

The rest of the nation were left to a prolonged wait for the forthcoming national elections where each aspirant was made to canvas his political muscle amongst his own tribe to contest and win that particular election.

Eventually, the nation became weary of the independent state if it meant no improvement at all in the lot of the majority's living standards. People were mostly interested in a new national leadership which identifies itself more closely with the local economy; they were more interested in a better management of local resources and an efficient distribution of income into the public sector, including education of their own children to improve their future.

In short, they needed a better understanding leadership which successfully and honestly manages both the economy and foreign policy.

Unfortunately, the civilian governments failed in both. When the Military Junta took over by the end of the 1st decade, the people were already ripe for an adventure of sorts, but they were not aware of what was in store for them.

Military dictatorship is what they did suffer from for the last three decades up to 1990. It is also what brought down the collapse of their national unity and government. They took ample advantage of the weakness inherent in a western democracy which could not be managed by civilian governments and seized power exercising every aspect of dictatorship and adventurism that was to be experienced by a poor state.

Now Somalia lies bare in tatters crying for a savior to provide a durable solution or a lasting formula.

For sure, that savior will not emerge from a foreign soil to suggest a magical prescription that may uplift the nation back to it feet. What most local politicians, even some warlords, liked others to hear was a grass roots solution.

What they all have failed to achieve is the grass roots solution in itself. Each one would like his piece of the meal cut out for him first. Then to hell with the rest. He may take the whole pie if possible for himself.

Yet an "inborn" or a home made solution shall always be better than a foreign one. It has already been mentioned or suggested somewhere else in this book that it remains for Somalis to clean up their own mess. No foreign government, be it international or regional, can come up with a viable solution. Everybody may have some vested interest to safeguard his own, of course.

That is the main reason all international or regional conferences held thus far have failed during the last decade. Others will fail too, if a comprehensive and totally agreed upon solution is not found among Somalis themselves. If they do not drop their hard feelings, bury the hatchet and shed hatred altogether, they will certainly fail too to live up to international community expectations.

But only a genuine Somali, well studied, and a comprehensive solution will live up to the name. When you attempt to survey the present Somali situation, the obvious picture which emerges is the fact that nearly most of the educated urban intelligentsia have migrated and are dispersed mostly in the west who accepted them in their midst as refugees.

Those who remained within the confines of the Somali borders are either the tribal diehards who battled all the consequences of a civil war over, or have been penniless or luckless to endure the hardship the whole nation suffered and is still undergoing despite a prolonged state of disarray and misery.

Bossaso town

International and regional conferences to bring the Somalis together have so far fell short of achieving a comprehensive solution which satisfies all factions.

The penultimate and most lengthy effort that has been made by a Somali neighbor, namely the current President of Djibouti Republic, and was recognized by the United Nations which reintroduced at least legal recognition to a hitherto nation failed state, have also fallen short of achieving Somali accord.

Both the Isaaq clan controlled Somaliland and the Darod clan controlled Puntland rejected the agreement reached in Djibouti. The present generation, in any case, has so far failed to finalize the Somali quagmire however. They could not overcome their shared hatred for each other and utterly failed to introduce remedying formulae of reconciliation. They still remain prisoners of their own tribal bias.

Therefore, the present generation, whether they are some of the protagonists, who may be calling the erratic shots occasionally or attending failed conferences, have thus far utterly failed to produce or to reach a lasting Somali solution.

With regard to the new generation, no one knows yet what solution they will come up with, but it is already known they are terribly dispersed and divided. The country cannot and will not easily accept any new idea, whether imported or not.

The Somali individual, who still lives his own traditional way, would welcome any peaceful idea, if it does mean a tangible progress of his living condition, or if it will eventually introduce him to a better way of life.

He will be happier if the urban part of the population pay more attention to and improve his way of life, whether in the nomadic areas or in the farming belt and plantation territory by the rivers side in the south of the country.

Not only that. He is ready to host a truly honest national administration which manages his affairs in a fair minded manner commensurate with his culture, provided that corruption, nepotism and graft are reduced to a minimum.

He is also willing to withstand hardship if it will lead him to a straight path of advancement and national harmony. He is more than willing to live with his neighbors in the event those neighbors respect their own identity and return unbiased territorial claims as a result of a total abandonment of further belligerence and brotherly hatred.

Experience and destruction taught him to work hard for his own survival. It also taught him the work ethic which is clearly spelled out in his faith.

This time around he has learned sufficiently from his historical lessons. No aspirant politician should dream of riding an imaginative idea of reaching a new Eldorado or a treasure trove full of riches at the expense of the poor masses. Wild ideas that are full of glitter might at first attract a crowd, but they will not produce a long term remedy for a chronically sick and corrupt economy.

In short, the Somali population is certainly ripe for a solution, but it is in dire need of a united, courageous and forward looking leadership that have a strong sense of mission and are determined to revive the nation in a genuine manner back to the right course of history.

Any drastic misstep in this regard could be highly catastrophic. Some down to earth political observers do foresee a practical solution and emphasize the fact, the surrounding world are interested to manipulate this quasi chaotic country for its own strategic aims.

They are influential and are only ready to work with powerful leaders who do not care about the fate of the populace more than their own interest of grabbing their self-centered aims of gaining power and enriching themselves and their own relatives.

Forget about them. Work hard to eliminate hatred and turn up a team of real Somalis, not tribes, clans or sub-clan minded junk. Only a team of sincere, people loving Somalis and with an honest and dedicated sense of mission can save this nation with several formulae or with one final genuine solution.

Who cares about these children?

Addendum

The reader shall come across a host of various abbreviations, acronyms or names that are attributed to either Somali fronts, political parties, tribes, international, regional or humanitarian organizations.

A casual reader may also find some of the tribal names and abbreviations which would require some specific knowledge rather confusing. Some brief explanatory notes will make matters easier for those who wish to understand the full meaning of same.

Listed are also some defunct political organizations which did play a pivotal or minor role in Somalia's march during its recent history toward independence.

Somali Major Political Outfits with Militia

Somali Salvation Democratic Front (SSDF)

A Darod clan controlled front with militia: Originally founded in the early seventies in Addis Ababa, Ethiopia, as a national front encompassing all Somali exiles under the leadership of Mustafa Haji Noor, a retired popular Radio Hargeisa and B.B.C. Somali Service broadcaster at the time under the name of the Somali Democratic Front (SODF), but was later changed to its present name of SSDF as stated in the heading.

Because of chronic divisiveness among its leadership it proved politically ineffective and gradually lost its nationalist appeal. However, when Col. Abdullahi Yusuf at the onset of the eighties defected to Ethiopia and took over the leadership of its military wing, a final split occurred among the Somali dissidents in the Diaspora.

Other tribally oriented fronts sprung in exile. After the fall of the Military dictatorship in Mogadishu, the SSDF re-emerged in the northern town of Garowe as a Darod clan front, headed by General Mohamed Abshir Musa who once served as the first national Police Commandant of independent Somalia.

Puntland was declared as a separate domestic territory, mostly inhabited by the Harti sub-clans group of the Darod. It refused to accept the outcome of the 2001 Djibouti Republic's hosted Somali Reconciliation Conference but declined secession and opted to remain within "Somalia proper".

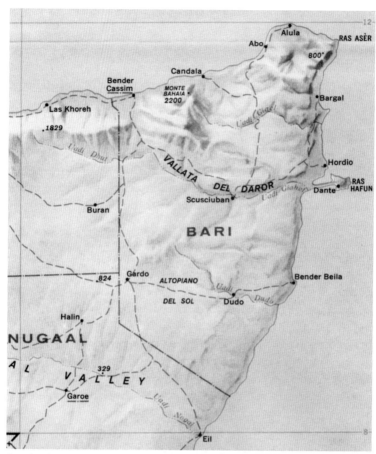

Puntland area

United Somali Congress (USC)

A Hawiye clan controlled front with militia: Began violent insurgency in the regions of Mudug, Galgudud, Hiran, Middle and Lower Shabelle and Banadir of southern Somalia in the mid eighties which culminated in the final uprising against Siad Barre's Military dictatorship in Mogadishu.

Led to its downfall on January 26th, 1991 and to the ensuing long drawn civil war. Divisiveness amongst the USC sub-clans only helped to prolong tribal conflict, eventually causing the demise of General Aideed, one of its famously belligerent leaders.

Somali National Movement (SNM)

An Isaaq clan controlled front with militia: Began violent insurgency in the north western regions of Woqoyi Galbed (Hargeisa, Berbera) and Tog Dheer (Bur'ao, Erigavo) and captured the regional Capitals of Hargeisa and Bur'ao for a while, prompting the Military Regime to unleash its fire power, including air raids and planting land mines, domestically killing and maiming unknown number of innocent civilians in the process.

Subsequent to the fall of the Siad Barre regime, the SNM unilaterally declared a secessionist republic in the north western regions of Somalia or the ex British Somaliland Protectorate which remains internationally unrecognized after more than a decade.

Rahanwein Revolutionary Army (RRA)

The only other major political force with militia in Somalia today is the Rahanwein Revolutionary Army of the Bay Region slightly northwest of Mogadishu.

After the fall of the Military dictatorship and the demise of General Aideed, the RRA emerged in the late nineties of the 20th Century and took over power in that region after forcing opposing fronts to flee. They subsequently began participating in Somali reconciliation conferences representing their region and its people. They still remain a power in that region and a main player in the politics of Somalia.

Smaller Fronts and Splinter Groups or Parties

Somali Patriotic Movement (SPM)

Originally created by Col. Ahmed Omer Jess who rebelled against the Military Regime in Hargeisa and went into exile in the mid eighties.

Overran Military garrisons in Bay and Ballidoogleh Airbase during January 1991.

Initially stopped in Afgoi for a while, but then settled in the southern port of Kismayo where he briefly reigned and declared his alliance with and support of General Aideed.

The SPM eventually split into two parts, when General Aden Noor Gabyow of the Awlyahan sub-clan of the Ogaden and General Mohamed Saeed Hersi, called "General Morgan", of the Mijertein sub-clan, a son-in-law of Siad Barre and his last Minister of Defense, entered the scene with other Darod clans and militia. Both created a rival SPM forcing Jess to flee Kismayo after few militia skirmishes.

General Aden Gabyow died recently, but Kismayo remains a disputed area suffering from a power vacuum like most of the rest of Somalia.

Somali National Front (SNF)

Originally headed by General Omer Haji Mohamed, a former Minister of Defense of Siad Barre. Represents the Marehan sub-clan of the Darod.

Somali Salvation National Movement (SSNM)

Represents the Dir clan. Was originally created by Col. Abdi Warsma Isaaq, a member of the Revolutionary Council (SRC) of the ousted Siad Barre Military Regime.

Somali African National Union (SANU)

A party representing the original Banadir Region's inhabitants.

Somali National Union (SNU)

A splinter party representing residents of Barawe on the Banadir southern coast. Emerged during the early period of the civil war.

United Somali Party (USP)

A defunct old alliance between the residents of Borama, Zeila, Las Anod and Las Koreh. Resurrected during the civil war early period by the Dholbahante and Warsangeli sub-clans of the Darod. Now absorbed politically by Puntland.

United Somali Front (USF)

Represented the Issa tribe, residing in Zeila in the early period of the civil war under the leadership of Mr. Abdurrahman Duaale.

Somali Youth League (SYL)

A defunct nationalist party which led the struggle toward independence in most parts of colonized Somali territories, especially in southern Somalia.

Somali Democratic Movement (SDM)
A defunct national party which focused its operations in the politics of the Bay Region.

International Forces and Organizations in Somalia

International forces which came to the rescue of the civilian Somali population, beleaguered at the time by famine and civil war, under the name of Operation Restore Hope, initiated by the United States Government but mainly operated under the umbrella of the United Nations Organization:

UNOSOM I or United Nations Organization Somalia Operation 1, April 1992 to March 1993

UNOSOM II or United Nations Organization Somalia Operation 2, March 1993 to March 1995

UNITAF or United Nations Task Force, Dec 1992 to May 1993. Introduced after the adoption of Resolution 814 of Chapter VII on March 1993 by the UNO Security Council.

Humanitarian Organizations
All participating humanitarian organizations, governmental as well as non-governmental (Non Governmental Organizations, NGO) who took part in the Somali rescue efforts were named under the Human Relief Sector (HRS).
   Some organizations retained their individual titles:
– International Committee of the Red Cross (ICRC)
– Organization of African Unity (OAU)
– Office of Foreign Disaster Assistance (OFDA), USAID
– Organization of the Islamic Conference (OIC)
– National Islamic Front (NIF)
– Somali Air Coordinating Body (SACB)

Somali Territory

Having outlined above most or all of the Somali political outfits and splinter groups, samples of hitherto published official versions of the current internationally recognized political and geographical maps were added, enabling the reader to have a fair idea of the territorial habitat of the Somali people. See maps on pages 6 and 129.

It must be pointed out, however, that the existing border which basically represents a partial union between only two out of five Somali parts, drawn throughout the European conference of 1885 at the behest of the new colonizers of the African continent during the 19th Century, is considered a de facto border and any recognition by former Somali governments or regimes was only dealing with existing facts on the political international arena in those times, but does not truly reflect the real dimensions of Somali territorial habitat which transcend those European imposed international border limits.

Genealogy of the Tribes in Somalia

Somali tribes are often mentioned in this script. The historically major tribes in Somalia are the Darod, the Isaaq and the Hawiye. For the purpose of our script, we may outline here below the various, sometimes significant sub-clans, either in the civil war or for playing a current or future role in forging a compromise or unity amongst indigenous tribes.

Tables of sundry tribal genealogies are also included to further exemplify the damaging effect of hold oral tradition may have on the Somali social psyche which is very important.

As already mentioned somewhere else in this book, lack of written historical records by earlier civilizations poses a real problem for any researcher or scholarly student of Somali roots. Oral history is more varied and less verifiable than written records.

At any rate, the author, himself a Somali, has taken an impartial approach to record the available oral stories about Somali tribal origins of all Somalis.

To be genuinely honest about the issue, one finds himself personally confused in the end for lack of reliable and conclusive information. One cannot depend on oral hearsay to determine the true ethnic background of an entire nation.

For that reason, the author chose to take contemporary Somalis as a parameter for racial homogeneity and decided to go along with the Hamitic background theory, agreeing with the description that Somalis are similar to other Cushitic speaking peoples in East and North Africa, including most Ethiopians, Djiboutians, Eritreans, Northeast Sudan's Beija peoples, Upper Egypt's Bashayira / Ababida and other Nubian tribes, also North African Berbers, the Tuareg tribe of the great Sahara desert and some Mauritanians. No matter how time and demographic movement may affect human habitat, their physical and linguistic features remain an authentic indicator of peoples' ethnic background.

Nevertheless, this choice or assumption remains only a theory, since no credible historical records were available to this author, especially on the level of influence of interbreeding with the Arabian migration to the Somali northern coastal areas; although in a recent survey, conducted by the British colonial authorities late in the 1940's of the 20th Century, they attributed the cause of that migration to a possible catastrophe, which might have probably upset the economic equilibrium in Arabia around the 10th Century and mentioning the probable arrival of the tribal patriarchs Darod and Isaaq respectively to the Somali northern coast villages of His and Mait during that period, according to the legend.

Systematics and Spelling

In the ensuing trees of tribes the number preceding a name indicates the generation in line of descent from the patriarch of the group; e.g. a name marked "4" is great-grandson of "1" and "7" is great-grandson of the next preceding "4".

Whereas in the preceding text names of tribes, clans and subclans as well as names of villages do not strictly follow the rules of either Somali or English spelling they are in the trees of tribes written the English way. Added names in [ ] indicate the Somali spelling.

In identical names vowels occasionally differ in writing. Instead of "e" sometimes "i" or "a" may occur, "o" may replace an "u" and vice versa. In the preceding text Banadir e.g. means the same as Benadir, Mijertein is identical to Majerteen, Mogadishu may be found as Muqdisho.

The Dominating Tribes

The DAROD [DAAROOD]

A Major clan that inhabits the Somali regions of Woqoyi Bari, Nugal, Mudug, Galgudud, Bakol, Gedo and Lower Juba of southern Somalia, as well as the Sol and Sanaag regions of northern Somalia. They also inhabit parts of the Howd area and the Ogaden region in Ethiopia and parts of the Northern Frontier District (NFD) of Kenya.

1. DAROD [DAROOD] (Abdurrahman Ismail) married a daughter of "Dir"
 2. SUHURRE Darod ⎯⎯⎯
 2. ESA Darod ... or ISE Darod [CIISE Darood]
 2. YUSUF Darod ... AURTOBLEH
 2. TANADLEH Darod
  3. LELKASEH Tanadleh
  3. KORSHE Tanadleh
  3. MALASMUGE Tanadleh
  3. FATAH Tanadleh
  3. LEGOD Tanadleh
  3. JUS Tanadleh
  3. ALAYE Tanadleh
 2. SEED Darod
  3. MAREHAN Seed
  3. FAHIA Seed
 2. MOHAMED Darod
  3. KUMADE Mohamed
   4. ABDI Kumade ... GELIMES
   4. ABSAME Kumade
    5. WETEN Absame
    5. BALAD Absame
    5. ABDEGALLA Absame
    5. OGADEN Absame
    5. WAK Absame

6. TAGAL Wak ... TAGALWAK

3. KOMBE Mohamed

  4. GARWEINE Kombe

  4. SALEBAN Kombe

  4. HAILE Kombe

  4. JIRAM Kombe

  4. JAMBEL Kombe

  4. GEH Kombe

  4. AMLALEH Kombe

   5. YABARAK Amlaleh

   5. GHERI Amlaleh

   5. HARTI Amlaleh

    6. MOHAMED Harti ... MIJERTEIN

    6. MAHAMUD Harti ... MURASANTE

     7. HINJIYEH Murasante

     7. MOHAMED Murasante ... WARSANGELI

     7. INJIH Murasante

     7. BAKANKE Murasante

      8. GOBIAWOOD Bakanke

      8. AUROMALE Bakanke

      8. OLMARARE Bakanke

    6. MURA ASSEH [MURA CASSEH] Harti AHMED

     7. DESHISHE [DESHIISHE] Mura Asseh

     7. KAPTANLEH Mura Asseh

     7. MAGANLABBE Mura Asseh

     7. TINLEH Mura Asseh

    6. KASKAGABE Harti

    6. LIBANGASHE Harti

    6. GESAGUL Harti ... GULED

    6. SEED Harti (MUSA) ... DHOLBAHANTE

The ISAAQ

A major clan who constitute the majority in the north western regions of Somalia. They mostly inhabit in the Woqooyi Galbeed, Togdheer and Sanaag Regions in Somalia and the Howd area that had been ceded to Ethiopia during 1954.

1. ISAAQ (Sheikh Ishaaq) [Sheikh Isxaaq]

2. IBRAAHIM Sheikh Ishaaq (HABAR HABUSHED [HABAR XABUUSHEED]) ... SAMBUR

2. MAHAMED Sheikh Ishaaq ... IBRAN [IBRAAN]

  3. ISE Mahamed [CIISE Maxamed]

  3. IGALLEH [CIGALLEH] Mahamed

  3. ABDALLE [CABDALLEH] Mahamed

   4. YONIS Abdalle

     5. ALI [CALI] Yonis

     5. KHAIR Yonis

   4. HASSAN Abdalle

   4. JIBRIL Abdalle

     5. UMAR [CUMAR] Jibril or OMAR Jibril

      6. BI'IDE [BICIIDE] Umar

      6. ISHAAQ [ISXAAQ] Umar

       7. AYUN [CAYUN] Ishaaq

       7. ALI [CALI] Ishaaq ... AFWEYNE

       7. URURSUGEH Ishaaq

     5. ABOKOR Jibril

      6. MAHAMED [MAXAMED] Abokor

       7. YESIF Mahamed

       7. ADAN Mahamed ... ADAN MADOBE [ADAN MADOOBE]

       7. NUR [NUUR] Mahamed

      6. SAMANEH Abokor

      6. MUSE Abokor

       7. UDURHMIN [UDURXMIIN] Muse

       7. IDRIS Muse

       7. ADARAHMAN [ADARAXMAAN] Muse

   4. BUTALEH Abdalle

   4. ADAN Abdalle

   4. HILDID [XILDID] Abdalle

   4. JIBRIL Abdalle

     5. UMAR Jibril

      6. BI'IDE Umar

      6. ISHAAQ Umar

       7. AYUN Ishaaq

       7. ALI Ishaaq ... AFWEYNE

       7. URURSUGEH Ishaaq

5. ABOKOR Jibril
  6. MAHAMED Abokor
    7. YESIF Mahamed
    7. ADAN Mahamed ... ADAN MADOBE
    7. NUH Mahamed
  6. SAMANEH Abokor
  6. MUSE Abokor
    7. UDURHMIN Muse
    7. IDRIS MUSE
    7. ADARAHMAN Muse
2. MUSE Sheikh Ishaaq ... HABAR HABUSHED [HABAR XABUUSHEED]
  3. MAHAMED Muse [MAXAMED Muuse]
  3. ABOKOR Muse
2. AHMED Sheikh Ishaaq ... Habitat: Tolje'lo [Toljeclo] and Region Galbee [Woqooyi Galbeed]
2. GARHEJIS [GARXEJIS] Sheikh Ishaaq
  3. SEED Garhajis ... HABAR YONIS
              (Missing link)
    5. ISHAAQ ARREH [ISXAAQ CARREH] ...
    Habitat: mostly between the villages of Bandar Wanaag (or Benderwanak*) on the old Hargeisa - Berbera gravel track in the north and Adaaley (or Adale*) close to the Hargeisa - Bur'ao road in the south.
    5. ISMA'IL ARREH [ISMAACIIL CARREH] Is'haaq
      6. MUSE Isma'il
      6. YONIS Isma'il ... SA'AD [SACAD] YONIS
      6. ABDALLE Isma'il ... MUSE ABDALLE
    5. MUSE ARREH
              (Missing links)
      11. ISMAN Hildid [CISMAAN XILDIID]
      (or OSMAN Hildid)
        12. HERSI Isman ... HERSI BARRE or AINANCHE
        12. ALI Isman ... BAH DULBAHANTE
      11. HUSEN Hildid [XUSEEN Xildiid] ... REER HUSSEIN

---

* Spelling used in the widely known Michelin road-map 954 of North East Africa, published 1988.

11. HASSAN Hildid [XASSAN Xildiid] … GUMBUR
3. DA'UD Garhajis [DAAUUD Garxajis] … IDAGALEH [CIIDAGALEH]
  4. MUSE Da'ud
  4. ISE [CIISE] Da'ud (or ISSE Da'ud)
  4. MAHAMED [MAXAMED] Da'ud
  4. BILAL [BILAAL] Da'ud
2. AYUB Sheikh Ishaaq
2. ARAB Sheikh Ishaaq
  3. ELI [CELI] Arab
  3. IDMAN Arab
  3. ABDALLE [CABDALLEH] Arab
2. AWAL Sheikh Ishaaq … HABAR AWAL
  3. SUBER [SUBEER] Awal
    4. MUSE Suber
     5. SA'AD [SACAD] Muse
      6. ABDURAHMAN Sa'ad [CABDURAXMAAN Sacad]
      6. HASSAN [XASSAN] Sa'ad
      6. ABDALLE [CABDALLE] Sa'ad
      6. ISAAQ Sa'ad
       7. ABOKOR Isaaq … REER SAMATAR
        8. JIBRIL Abokor
       7. YASIF Isaaq … REER LIBAN
       7. MAKAHIL [MAKAAHIIL] Isaaq
     5. ISE Muse (or ISSE Muse)
      6. ADAN Ise [Ciise]
       7. JIBRIL Adan
      6. ABOKOR Ise
      6. MAHAMED [MAXAMED] Ise
       7. HASSAN Mahamed
       7. JIBRIL Mahamed
      6. IDRIS [IDRIIS] Ise
    5. AFGAB [AFGAAB] Muse (Habitat: scattered among other HABAR AWAL sub-clans)
    5. ELI [CELI] Muse (Habitat: scattered among other HABAR AWAL sub-clans)
    5. IGALLEH [CIGALLEH] Muse (Habitat: scattered among other HABAR AWAL sub-clans)

5. ABDALLE [CABDALLE] Muse (Habitat: scattered among other HABAR AWAL sub-clans)

The HAWIYE

A major clan which mainly inhabits the central regions of Mudug, Galgudud, Hiran, Middle and Lower Shabelle, Banadir, parts of Bay and Upper and Lower Juba and parts of the Ogaden of Ethiopia and the NFD of Kenya beyond the presently recognized Somali borders. It is mainly composed of HIRAB, KARANLE, GUGUNDHABE, and HAWADLE.*

They included other sub-clans that were not considered as part of the Hawiye well before the civil war, such as the SHEIKHAL.* *

The AJURAN and DAGODIA [DAGOODIA] sub-clans appeared as supporters of the HAWIYE during the civil war. The major warring sub-clans then were HABAR GIDIR (General Aideed) and ABGAL (Ali Mahdi).

The MUDULOD, who are also mentioned in the book, are a group of clans who were allied to the ABGAL and supported them during the civil war. They include the ODAJEN, MOBLEN, WA'DAN, and HILLIBEY.

1. HAWIYE
 2. KARANLE Hawiye
  3. GIDIR Karanle

---

* The HAWADLE sub-clan does not feature in the HAWIYE tribal tree since he was a maternal son and the genealogy is paternal. He is a HAWIYE by virtue of being brought up by his mother and growing up prior to proliferation as a sub-clan amongst his maternal relatives.

** The SHEIKHAL tribal identity remains confusing. The word MARTILE, which means 'guest', has a dubious connotation attached to it. Some Somalis believe that it has been devised by certain SHEIKHAL tribal elders allied with the HAWIYE clan uprising for political reasons. Some Somalis believe the southern Somalia sub-clan of the SHEIKHAL 'LO BOGAY' are convinced they are part of the HAWIYE clan, whilst the northern SHEKHAL 'AW QUDBI' might be part of another Somali clan. Some SHEIKHAL, mainly living in the coastal village of Al Jazeera south of Mogadishu and are called 'SHEKHAL GENDERSHE', are believed to be an extension of the GELEDI tribe which is part of the RAHANWEIN alliance of DIGIL and MIRIFLEH, residing in the Regions of Bay, Bakol and Lower Shabelle.

3. SAHAWLEH [SAXAWLEH] Karanle

3. WADHERE [WAADHEERE] Karanle … MURUSADE [MURUSADE]

  4. MURUSADE Wadhere [Waadheere]

    5. SABTI Murusade

    5. FOL'ULUS [FOOLCULUS] Murusade

2. HASKUL [XASKUL] Hawiye

2. RARANE [RARAANE] Hawiye

2. GURGATE [GURGAATE] Hawiye

 3. DAMAY [DAAMAY] Gurgate

  4. HIRAB [HIRAAB] Damay

    5. MUDULOD [MUDULOOD] Hirab

      6. DARANDOLLE [DARANDOOLLE] Mudulod

       7. HILLIBEY [HIILLIBEY] Darandolle

       7. USMAN Darandolle

        8. ALI Usman … ABGAL [ABGAAL]

         9. HARTI Ali (Abgal)

         9. WA'BUDHAN [WACBUUDHAN] Ali (Abgal)

         9. WA'AYSLEH [WACAYSLEH] Ali (Abgal)

        8. MOBLEN [MOBLEEN] Usman

        8. WA'DAN [WACDAAN] Usman

        8. ILABAY Usman

      6. ISE [CIISE] Mudulod … ODAJEN (or OJAJEN)

      6. WA'WEYTEEN [WACWEYTEEN] Mudulod

     5. MAHAMOUD Hirab … DUDUBLE

     5. MADARKI'IS [MADARKICIS] Hirab … HABAR GIDIR

      6. SA'AD [SACAD] Madarki'is

      6. AYR [CAYR] Madarki'is

      6. SALEBAN [SALEBAAN] Madarki'is

      6. SARUR [SARUUR] Madarki'is

     5. MARTILE Hirab … SHEKHAL

2. GUGUNDHABE Hawiye

 3. BADI ADDE [BAADI CADDE] Gugundhabe

 3. JEJELLE [JEJEELLE] Gugundhabe

 3. JIDLEH Gugundhabe

2. JAMBELLE Hawiye

2. SIL'IS [SILCIS] Hawiye

2. WADALAN Hawiye

The HAWADLE, a sub-clan inhabiting the Region of Hiran, is believed to have been originally a maternal son of the HAWIYE. According to oral tradition it is believed by the HAWIYE that he was brought up in his infancy by one of his immediate uncles, namely ISE (ODAJEN) Mudulod. Although the HAWADLE outnumber the ISE as a sub-clan in the HIRAN Province until today, members of the HAWADLE still call the ISE traditionally as uncles. Both live together in the Hiran Region.

The SAMARON or GADABURSI [GADABUURSI]

1. SAMARON
   2. ISE [CIISE] SAMARON ... part of HABAR AFFAN*
   2. YUSUF SAMARON ... part of HABAR AFFAN [CAFFAAN]
   2. SUBER [SUBEER] SAMARON ... part of HABAR AFFAN
      3. MAHAMED [MAXAMED] Suber ... DHEGAWEYNE
      3. MAKAHIL [MIKAAHIIL] Suber
         4. MUSE Makahil
         4. ELI [CELI] Makahil
         4. IGEH [CIGEH] Makahil
         4. HASSAN [XASSAN] Makahil ... BA HABAR HASSAN
         4. ABDALLAH [CABDALLAH] Makahil ... BA HABAR ABDALLAH
            5. KAMIS Abdallah [Cabdallah] ... part of BA SAMARON
      3. MUSE Suber
   2. MIKADORE [MIKADOORE] SAMARON
      3. MAKAHIL Mikador
      3. MAHAD ASSEH [CASSEH] Mikador
         4. ADAN Mahad Asseh [Casseh] ... BA HABAR ADAN, part of BA SAMARON
         4. ABOKOR Mahad Asseh ... BA HABAR ABOKOR
            5. BARRE Abokor ... part of BA SAMARON
            5. ABDALLE [CABDALLAH] Abokor ... part of BA SAMARON

---

* Four sub-clans, namely HEIJIRREH, JIBRAIN, ALI GANUN [CALI GANUUN] and GOBO who are parallel to the SAMARON have been conveniently attached to the HABAR AFFAN group of SUBER, YUSUF and ISE SAMARON.

5. SEED Abokor

4. HUSSEIN [XUSSEIN] Mahad Asseh ... BA HABAR ELI

4. MUSE Mahad Asseh

  5. SA'AD [SACAD] Muse ... HASSAN SA'AD

  5. FIN Muse ... MUSE FIN

  5. HAMUD [XAMUD] Muse ... REER HAMUD

  5. ADAN Muse ... FAROLEH

  5. MAKAHIL DHERE [MAKAHIIL DHEERE] Muse

  5. JIBRIL Muse ... AFGUDUD [AFGUDUUD]

  5. MAHAMED [MAXAMED] Muse ... part of
BA SANYARO

  5. MUSE Muse ... part of BA SANYARO

  5. IDRIS Muse ... part of BA SANYARO

  5. YONIS Muse ... part of BA SANYARO

   6. NUR Yonis ... REER NUR

   6. ALI Yonis

   6. ADAN Yonis

   6. JIBRIL Yonis

The RAHANWEIN

1. RAHANWEIN

 2. DIGIL Rahanwein

  3. JIDO* [JIIDO] Digil

  3. TUNNI Digil

  3. GELEDI Digil

  3. GOBRON [GOOBROON] Digil

  3. QURABANE [QURAABANE] Digil

  3. GARRE Digil

  3. GALADLEH Digil

  3. BAGADI Digil

 2. MIRIFLEH Rahanwein

  3. ELAI Mirifleh

  3. LESAN [LEESAAN] Mirifleh

  3. HARIEN Mirifleh

  3. JILIBLEH Mirifleh

  3. YANTAR [YANTAAR] Mirifleh

  3. QOMAL [QOOMAAL] Mirifleh

* Larger sub-clans are underlined.

3. HADAMO Mirifleh
3. GASSAR GUDDE Mirifleh
3. MA'ALINWEYNE [MACALINWEYNE] Mirifleh
3. HELLEDA Mirifleh
3. LUWAI Mirifleh
3. DABARRE Mirifleh
3. HUBER [HUBEER] Mirifleh
3. JAMBAULUL Mirifleh
3. DISOW Mirifleh
3. BARBARO [BARBAARO] Mirifleh
3. EYLO
3. GABAWEYN
3. ASHRAF
3. EMAD
3. GARAWLE
3. REER DUMAL
3. HEROW
3. WANJEL
3. SHANTA ALEMOD or Five Leaves

The RAHANWEIN were originally composed of 17 sub-clans in a loose alliance. They almost totally occupy the Region of Bay and partly reside in the Regions of Bakol and Lower Shabelle.

They eventually increased in numbers and reached up to 33 sub-clans including the major ones. Their exact number is currently unknown. With the existing chaotic situation in Somalia, it is almost impossible to carry out any form of statistical compilation.

The people who live in these regions endured the most devastating effects of famine and banditry at the break out of civil war there.

They were formed more than two centuries ago basically from most of the northern nomadic clans of ISAAQ, DAROD and HAWIYE throughout their continuous migration southward in search of more grazing territory. Subsequently, they were increased by an influx of Asians and probably a tiny European settlement, which were totally assimilated but some of whom may have retained certain elements of a separate subculture within their localities.

For instance the people of Barawe (which probably was called Brava and may have been visited by the famous maritime explorer

Vasco da Gama) still speak the local dialect, which is more identifiable with the archaic Zanzibari Kiswahili, as well as the main Somali dialect.

The RAHANWEIN made it a condition on new residents in the Bay Region to cease any claims of prior tribal ancestry once they join the RAHANWEIN alliance. Only one Somali clan, namely the DIR and two sub-clans of the MIJERTEIN and HABAR GIDIR declined to abandon their tribal identity for the sake of a RAHAN-WEYNE one.

One may find descendants of Portuguese sailors in the coastal village of Barawe on the Indian Ocean's Banadir coast, which was later ruled by the Omani Sultan of Zanzibar during the 19th Century along with Merca and Mogadishu before the Italians bought it from him.

In Mogadishu's oldest quarters of Hamar Wein, Shangaani and Shibbis one would encounter some pockets of settlements, featuring the cosmopolitan characteristic of the old Indian Ocean Port.

There is also a locally pronounced concentration of BAJUNI elements of the BESHA SHANAD, who are probably remnants of Omani fishermen or sailors who settled in Kismayo and the Lower Juba coastal area during the Zanzibari Sultanate reign over the East African Swahili coast.

The ISE MADOBE [CIISE MADOOBE] or ESA
1. ISE MADOBE … ESA
 2. HAULA GATE Esa … WALALDON [WALAALDOON]
  3. MAKAHIR [MAKAAHIIR] Haula Gate
  3. IDLEH Haula Gate
  3. MAHAMUD Haula Gate
   4. HASSAN Mahamud [XASSAN Maxamud]
   4. ABOKOR Mahamud
    5. YUSUF Abokor
    5. ALI Abokor
     6. HALAS Ali
     6. AHMED Ali
     6. BAHAR Ali
     6. BINLEH Ali
 2. HOLLEH Esa … FORLABE

3. MAHADLEH Holleh
  4. BIRBOREH [BIRBOOREH] Mahadleh
  4. ABOKOR Mahadleh
    5. ARREH Abokor
    5. ALI Abokor
    5. FARAH Abokor
    5. ALIJIRREH Abokor
    5. HASSAN Abokor
3. SAHIB [SAAXIIB] Holleh
  4. AHMED Sahib [AXMED Saaxib]
  4. ELI [CELI] Sahib
    5. ABOKOR Eli
    5. HARUN Eli
    5. ELI Eli
    5. GABAR Eli
      6. IDLEH Gabar
        7. ABOKOR Idleh
2. ILEYE [ILEEYE] Esa
  3. MAMASAN Ileye [Ileeye]
    4. UMAR [CUMAR] Mamasan
    4. HASSAN [XASSAN] Mamasan
    4. AWR Mamasan
  3. MUSE Ileye
    4. MOHORREH Muse
    4. BIDEH Muse
    4. SA'AD [SACAD] Muse

No information was found concerning the clans of
– URWEYNE [UURWEINE]
– HORONE [XOROONE] and
– WARDIKH.

The IRIR or IRIR SAMALEH RAM NAG
1. IRIR ... IRIR SAMALEH RAM NAG
  2. DIR
  2. MADOBE [MADOOBE]
  2. HAWIYE
  2. BIYOMAL [BIYOMAAL]

2. AJURAN [AJUURAAN]
2. GALJE'EL [GALJECEEL]
2. DAGODIA [DAGOODIA]
  3. ISE [CIISE] ... ESA
  3. SAMARON [SAMAROON]

IRIR SAMALEH [SAMAALEH] is the great grandson of a possibly pre Somali Abyssinian , called RAM NAG who is nicknamed as the wealthy in Somali oral lore. Unfortunately no credible written history was recorded at the appropriate time; hence the subsequent confusion in the Somali race's authentic origin.

Some anthropologists claimed, the Somali people's migration began from the southwest to the Horn of Africa ages ago.

Others claimed the fact that most major current Somali patriarchs were buried in the Somali north eastern coastal village of Mait (ISSAQ, ESA, SAMARON and HALLAYA of the DAROD) near Badhan by the Al hills points to a circumstantial evidence that there existed a large Somali settlement in this relatively fertile area.

The same area, being coastal facing the south Arabian Gulf of Aden, could have been a convenient ground for interracial breeding.

There are also some historical traces and logical assumptions that migration in search of a larger grazing territory led to an opposite migratory pattern, which prompted Somali nomads travelling with their livestock to move toward both, the south and southwest in the savannah until they were stopped by either other competing forces or by nature.

Both theories might be historically correct if they agree to adjust their timing to reflect the correct epoch.

DAROD or Abdirahman Ismail Ghabarti [Cabdraxmaan Ismaaciil Ghabarti], according to a British colonial authority survey of the 1940's, was one of the patriarchs who came one month earlier than Sheikh Isahac to the Somali eastern coastal village of His from Arabia.

He could have originally hailed from the GHABART tribal area situated in the highlands north of Addis Ababa, where the GHABART tribe lived for ages, although his grave may still be found at the town of Zabid in the Yemen.

It is historically recorded that Tigrinean monarchs of Axum did rule the Yemen or 'Arabia Felix' as it was called in ancient times.

Yemeni rulers did reign over Abyssinia as well in old times. There was a historical hint in the claim Emperor Haile Selassie of Ethiopia always used to make evident that his throne was linked to the biblical Queen Sheba of the Yemen.

It was also a known fact that many Arabic words are included in the current Amharic vocabulary.

The BESHA SHANAD [BEESHA SHANAAD]

"BESHA SHANAD" which means "the fifth group of sub-clans" represents all the minority sub-clans or groups in Somali society, including Bantus, Barawans and lower casts.

They have only recently been added to the list of clans and given seats in the new Federal Somali Parliament which is being formed in Nairobi, Kenya during the conclusive stage of the Somali Reconciliation Conference each according to its size and influence. Its intention is to secure their participation within the political process of rebuilding the Somali nation.

Their representatives were with the first batch of members of the new Parliament and were sworn in in the UNO Regional Office in Nairobi in mid August 2004.

BESHA SHANAD sub-clans and groups:

- JARER WEYNE, some of the Somali Bantus.
- BANADIR, original Banadir coast citizens particularly in Mogadishu and Merca.
- MEHERI, a Somali sub-clan which traces its origin to the MAHARA tribe of South Yemen or the Island of Socatra near Cape Gardafui of the Indian Ocean. Lives with MIJERTEIN, especially with coast sub-clans
- RER AW HASSAN, Somali sub-clan.
- MADHIBAN, the most common name of all Somali low cast sub-clans.
- YAHAR [YAXAR], a Somali lower cast sub-clan in the region of Hiran. They are regarded as equivalent of the YIBIRs in Northern Somalia.
- AJURAN, Somali sub-clan, lives mostly in Ethiopia and Kenya.
- ARAB SOMALI or Somali Arabs or Yemenis.
- GAR JANTE, Somali sub-clan.

- YIBIR, Somali lower cast sub-clan. Live as sorcerers with all tribes, in particular with MIJERTEIN.
- MUSE DHERI or MUSE DIRIYEH, Somali lower cast sub-clan.
- BARAWAN, citizens of the Banadir coast town of Barawe (or Brava). There are two components. The TUNNIS are dark skinned and form the majority in the area including the hinterland. The township BARAWANIS are fair skinned and live within the coastal port of Barawe. They are part of the RAHAN-WEIN alliance.
- BAJUNI, citizens of Kismayo port and neighbouring villages.

Other Sundry Small Clans and Sections

- AYUB SHEIKH ISAHAQ, with the HABAR AWAL sub-clan DAAD MUSE, Hargeisa.
- AKISHU, with the HABAR AWAL sub-clan AHMED ABDULLAH, Hargeisa.
- WARAMIYO - HASSAN
- WARAKIYO - 'ALI
- IGU – ?
- HAWIYE REER FIQASHINI, with Nogal DOLBAHANTE.
- REER DOD, with HABAR sub-clan MOHD. ABOKOR, Bur'ao.
- HINJINLEH, ? Pre-Somali, with DOLBAHANTE sub-clan BIH IDRAIS, Erigavo.
- MAGADLEH, ? Pre-Somali, with DOLBAHANTE sub-clan BIH IDRAIS, Erigavo.
- JIBRAHIL, ? Pre-Somali, Erigavo, some also with REER HERSI AINANSHE, Bur'ao.
- GEHAILE, ? MIJERTEIN or Pre-Somali, Erigavo.
- TURYER, live with DOLBAHANTE and MUSE ABOKOR, Erigavo.
- LO JIR, Pre-Somali and some GURGURREH with WARSANGELI sub-clan OMAR, Erigavo
- BARTIRE ba SHEIKHASH, with HABAR -YUNIS sub-clan MUSE ABDALLE, sub-clan FARAH MOHAMED, Berbera.
- ABASGUL, some with DOLBAHANTE ba ARARSAME.
- MIDGAN, Pre-Somali, MUSE DERIEH and MADIBAN, live as hunters and leather workers with all tribes.
- TOMAL, Pre-Somali, Blacksmiths, live with all tribes.
- ZEILAWI, very mixed race of the ancient city of Zeila.

As no significant or credible archives of latter statistical data reflecting demographic changes were safely kept for the last two decades, one remains at a loss to gather any reliable information concerning Somali tribal movement or population of recent times.

If the author attempt to record all the clans and sub-clans and their derivatives or various lineages it may detract us from the core subject of our script. However, what is described above would suffice our purposes or desire for the present. Let us hope, we remain sufficiently elucidated that tribal accord and peaceful coexistence remains the essential grass root ingredient for peace within the Somali Society.

About the Author

Hassan Ali Jama: Born in Berbera, Somaliland, February 1942. Grew up and completed secondary education in Aden, Yemen. Worked briefly as a civil servant with the British Administration during the first half of the 1960's. Also contributed in his youth to "Alyaqdha", an Arabic daily newspaper in Aden in support of the Somali movement for independence and unification.

Moved to Mogadishu, the Capital of Somalia, in the latter years of the 1960's where he briefly managed an export-import business until the advent of the Somali Military take over in 1969.
Joined Somali Airlines in 1970 as an employee to eventually become Traffic Manager. Resigned in 1982.

Established own Travel and Trading Agency early 1983. Represented Lufthansa, German Airlines and acted as a consultant for Boeing Commercial Airplane Company among others in Somalia until January 1991.

Fleeing national hostilities moved with his family to Cairo, Egypt, after the breakout of the Somali Civil War and the ouster of the Military Dictatorship.

Now lives in the United States with members of his own family as a refugee.